REVIEWE

D0469184

*T*ell all the guys who wri
life to watch out. Mallory Burton is a woman who can fish
with any of them and who writes better. She knows more
than fish and streams and tackle; she knows the hearts and
minds of the humans who are happiest when they are waist-
deep in a wild river.
Steven Bodio, reviewer, *Fly Rod & Reel* magazine

*W*hether the essay is humorous or serious, Mallory's
writing will take you deeper into the waters of flyfishing than
just catching fish. She is one of the most talented and creative
angling writers today.
Marty Sherman, editor, *Flyfishing* magazine

*M*allory Burton is just what flyfishing needs — a writer
with the wit and humor to lighten our sport's heavier load of
instructional literature. I read her with complete enjoyment.
**Maxine Egan, two-time winner of the Lillian
Sparrow Trophy, Tyee Club of British Columbia**

*N*o doubt about it, Mallory Burton is a writer, and the
fraternal order of anglers is fortunate that she chooses them
as her subjects.
**Van Egan, author and fishing buddy to Roderick
Haig-Brown**

*A*s a fisher, Mallory Burton stands on her own with anyone.
As a writer, she's a female John Gierach: with great clarity,
she gives the details of everyday life and flyfishing. When she
calls them forth, you know why you are alive and why you
fish.
Dennis Breer, guide on the Green River, Utah

AUG   1996

Reading the Water

Stories and Essays of Flyfishing and Life

by
Mallory Burton

"A Guide's Advice," "The Facts," "The Firehole," "Richard Said That," "Geoffrey's Wife," "Fishing With the Boys," "A Salmon Journal," "Messing With the River Gods," "Timing the Strike," "The Microscopic Optic," "Night Fishing" and "The Fence Pool Shark" were all published previously in *Flyfishing* (1989-95). "Bloodknots,""Droppers," "Rattlers" and "The Spent Fish Conversation," were previously published in *The Flyfisher* (1990-94). "Why I Never Fish in British Columbia" and "The Emerger" were published in *Flyfishing News, Views & Reviews* (1990). "The Virtual Angler" was published in *Fly Rod & Reel* (1994). "Mentors" was published in *Uncommon Waters*, 1991. Parts of "Raising the Profile: Women Who Fish," originally published in *Shimano Catalog* (1994), were incorporated into "Fishing With the Boys."

Keokee Co. Publishing, Inc.
P.O. Box 722
Sandpoint, ID 83864
Phone: (208) 263-3573

Printed on recycled paper

Printed in Canada
10 9 8 7 6 5 4 3 2 1

Library of Congress Cataloging-in-Publication Data
Burton, Mallory, 1952 -
Reading the water: stories and essays of flyfishing and life / by Mallory Burton.
          p.   cm.
ISBN 1-879628-10-4 (pbk.)
          1. Fishing stories, American. 2. Fly fishing–Fiction.
3. Outdoor life–Fiction. 4. Fly fishing. 5. Outdoor life.
I. Title.
PS3552.U775R43   1995
813'.54–dc20   95-14838 CIP

CONTENTS

To
Grandma Laine and Papa Ed
for the gifts
of art and flyfishing

Introduction

I FIRST HAD THE PLEASURE of reading Mallory Burton's work while editing a collection of women's fishing literature in 1990. Discovering her work was like stumbling onto a spring creek I'd never before fished — sparkling and full of potential — and I couldn't believe I hadn't found it earlier. Teeming with new insights, and chock full of fishing finesse, Mallory Burton's work has entertained angling devotees for years and added dimension and humor to flyfishing's trade magazines. *Reading the Water*, her first book, is a choice compendium of essays and stories and a wonderful addition to the literature of flyfishing.

Joining a small handful of angling books written by women, *Reading the Water* features women, men and children whose lives are influenced by, or sometimes steeped in, angling's antics and allure. Much of Mallory Burton's writing explores the lives of fishing women: a single mother who helps her son to realize the awe and grace of flyfishing, an outdoorswoman who stashes a dead rattler in her hat; a grieving daughter; a wise guide;

a new brand of fishing widow; a high-spirited angling hustler named Brook E. Trout.

While Mallory Burton's work shares the humor, renewal and adventure that marks all good angling literature, her perspective as a woman offers something more: a tapestry of multi-layered lives in which the landscape of emotion, the textures of love and relationships, and the choices, struggles and joys around family are woven throughout the experience of flyfishing.

Men who dip into *Reading the Water* will surely be entertained — they might even think twice about what tactic to take next time they come across a woman midstream. As Mallory Burton observes: "Unlike fish, men do not always disappear obligingly when you let them go." But readers will find much more than quips; the stories here also delve into the lives of men and boys — young men searching for their potential, older men coming to terms with theirs; an excessively attentive guide; a businessman and neophyte angler who looks to angling to save his life.

"Dinner at Charley's" and "The Virtual Angler" display a refreshing style and imagination while breaking new ground in the genre. "Dinner at Charley's" offers a good-natured parody of the work of one of flyfishing's best known writers. ("With apologies to Ernest Schweibert, of course.") And "The Virtual Angler" presents a futuristic romp into angling in the next millennium in which descendants of flyfishing's forebears meet their heritage in a very high-tech fashion.

Sure to bring a knowing smile to the face of any seasoned angler are the essays and vignettes included here about the foibles and delights of flyfishing. Among the topics deftly tackled are the many meanings of "Bait," the nobility of the salmon and the treachery of snakes. Mallory Burton's commitment to conservation and her strong connection to the natural order resonate throughout both her fiction and nonfiction. Flyfishing purists will undoubtedly see their angling lives reflected back at them through the prose of a writer who shares their passions for and dedication to the sport.

As the daughter of a fishing guide (though he wasn't a flyfisher), Mallory Burton was handed a rod and reel early in life. But 15 years ago she tossed aside the last of her bait and took up flyfishing under the tutelage of two friends who led her to the famed waters of the Henry's Fork for her baptism — but only after she proved to them she could cast to hit a beer can at 45 feet. A woman who now doesn't let a week go by without finessing salmon, steelhead or cutthroat in her native British Columbia and who spends entire summers exploring the roiling waters of the American West (and then winters writing about them for *Fly Rod and Reel*, *Flyfishing* and *The Flyfisher*), Mallory Burton brings a lifetime of fishing experience to *Reading the Water*.

Whether offering a dose of humor, a valuable bit of technique, or a reading of dangerous currents beneath the surface of our lives and relationships, each of the two dozen stories in this wonderful first collection will charm your angler's soul and perhaps inspire you from the armchair into the waters themselves.

Holly Morris
Seattle, Washington

Part I

Cut Banks

Nick did not want to go in there now. He felt a reaction against deep wading with the water deepening up under his armpits, to hook big trout in places impossible to land them.

— Ernest Hemingway
"Big Two-Hearted River"

Reading the Water

A Guide's Advice

I'VE ROWED FOR WOMEN BEFORE. A few were fluffs, good-natured types who attempted a couple of casts, fussed dutifully over their husbands' fish, and went back to reading their novels. A few were outright maniacs, fishing like troopers from dawn to dark-thirty, so jazzed about the river I worried they'd cash in their return tickets for one more day on the water. But most of the women I take out on the river these days are just dedicated anglers, outfishing the men in the boat because they can take a guide's advice without their egos getting in the way.

Rebecca Sheffield, well, she was a different type altogether. And she had reasons all her own for being on the river. She booked the trip six months ago. I remember taking that call. Andy, the owner, usually handles the bookings for the shop, but he was off bonefishing somewhere — hard to pin that guy down — and I was filling in. There wasn't much happening that day. I had a fire going in the woodstove and the coffee on. Usually you can count on a few of the regulars to come by for a chat, but that day nobody showed up. I'd spent most of the day sorting out the fly bins, so I was happy to take a few calls.

The conversation stood out among the others because it was so sparse, so impersonal. Most clients are anxious to chat it up, to pick your brain with questions about the water conditions and the bugs and gear. Ms. Sheffield just asked for a solo day trip on July 15. You would have thought she was booking the trip for someone else. Or maybe she fished so often, the whole thing had become routine. I hadn't been working out of Andy's shop for very long, and I wasn't all that familiar with his clientele. On the off chance that she was one of our repeat clients, I asked her who she'd like to float with.

"Are you free?" she asked.

"According to the book, I am."

"I'll fish with you then." I jotted her name in the book.

"I'd be happy to take you out. I'm Paul Martin by the way."

She hung up.

Middle of March we had one of those freak Montana snowstorms that pretty well shuts down the town. Andy thought it might be a good time to put together some of the mail orders that were piling up and confirm a few trips. He'd only been back from Belize a couple of days, and I remember walking in out of the cold and thinking how out-of-place the guy looked in his own shop. I don't mean to suggest there's anything funny-looking about Andy. He's a real good-looking guy — tall, strong enough to handle a boat no problem. But there he was with this perfect tan in the middle of winter, hair sun-bleached white-blond, and these clean, clean fingernails. Strictly Hollywood. Dye his hair black, stick him on a horse, and he could be the Marlboro Man. Didn't even get my boots off and already he's down to business. That's the Easterner coming out in him, I guess.

"Who took this one?" he wanted to know. There was a big red line under Rebecca Sheffield in the book.

"I did. Not the friendliest gal. You know how those Easterners are."

"Coming alone?"

"Assume so. She didn't mention anyone else."

"Let me know how it goes."

"Want me to confirm her?"

"No. Just curious. We don't get many women fishing alone."

We never did confirm the trip, and we didn't hear from her again until last night, when she called from her motel. I suggested we meet at the shop in the morning, around eight.

"Perhaps you could pick me up here," she said, "on your way out."

She was obviously new at this, or maybe she just didn't like any fuss. Meeting at the shop was a big part of the ritual, all the guides and the clients trading stories and sizing each other up.

"No trouble at all. How're you fixed for gear?"

"I don't have any flies," she said.

I laughed. "That's the beauty of flyfishing. You can

have your vest stuffed full of fly boxes and still never have exactly the right fly."

"I don't have any," she repeated.

"Better bring lots of money, then," I warned. "The Beaverhead willows have been known to eat a few flies."

"Of course," she said.

As it turned out, Rebecca Sheffield looked like she could afford to lose a few flies. Maybe a lot of flies. I couldn't say why. Maybe it was her New England accent and reserve, or the way she held herself, so straight and confident. She wasn't flashy, but she was attractive, classic even. Her straight brown hair was pulled back off her face and tied with a thin ribbon. She didn't wear perfume or jewelry. She was fine-boned, but square-jawed and long-legged, which gave her an athletic appearance. You could picture her in jodhpurs sailing over a stone fence or stalking through a meadow with a bird dog heeled at her side and a little Browning bent over her arm.

"Ms. Sheffield," I said, as she came over to the pickup.

"Rebecca," she said. We shook hands.

We loaded her gear and headed out on the old highway. Rebecca sat quietly, looking out the window.

"We'll put in near the Tash ranch," I told her, "and float all the way back into town. The shuttle vehicle's parked near the city dump. You might say we're floating Tash to trash."

If Rebecca wasn't a sparkling conversationalist, at least she had boat manners. She stayed clear while I loaded and launched the Avon. And I didn't have to keep an eye on her. Some clients wander around in the sage, and you have to remind them about the snakes. Rebecca just stood in one spot on the bank, staring out at the water. She rinsed the soles of her wading boots before she stepped into the raft.

I got a good look at the single flyrod she had brought as we shoved off. It was a custom job on a top-quality blank, set up in a style that was popular maybe two, three years ago. It looked familiar, quite a bit like the rods that Andy used to build when he first opened the shop. I wouldn't have been surprised to see his logo on the shaft.

"Nice rod," I said. "How's it fish?"

"I don't know," she answered. "I've had some casting lessons, that's all. The rod was a gift."

"Well, most of the casting's close in here," I assured her. "If you can manage thirty feet with any accuracy, you'll catch fish. Don't worry."

"I won't," she said.

I didn't doubt it for a minute.

On those rare occasions when I take out a solo trip, I like to float the lower third of the river. The fish are a bit smaller there, but more plentiful, or maybe just more visible. The banks are closer together, making it difficult for two anglers to fish simultaneously without getting in each other's way. But it's perfect for one client. The willows are overgrown, and the casting distances are short.

I shipped the oars and let the boat drift through the first bend. The river narrowed to 20 feet, the overhanging trees barely allowing the boat's passage. I grabbed a handful of silvery-green willow branches and pulled us through, hand over hand. The willows' exposed roots were bleached the color of barnwood. They reached down toward the water, casting shadows that were nearly indistinguishable from the long, dark shapes of the trout lying in their shade. As the boat approached, the shadows of the willows slowly dissolved. The shadows that were fish bolted from their cover and fled downriver ahead of us. The river took another turn, and the boat emerged from the willows. A dozen fish suddenly streaked from beneath the undercut bank and raced downstream.

About this time, the more romantic clients start murmuring rubbish about the "African Queen" or some other exotic river saga. The more practical ones just grab for their rods. It's generally all I can do to convince them that the better water is yet to come — that we've still got some rowing to do if we want to catch the hatch just right.

If Rebecca had seen any of the fish we kicked out, she gave no indication. She sat motionless on the front casting seat, every inch as cool and deep as the river.

After a few hundred yards, the channel widened enough to allow a reasonable casting margin. I pulled in behind a gravel bar and rigged Rebecca's rod. The leader was old and brittle; it came apart in my hands. I replaced it and tied on a small dun. I shook out the leader and handed her the rod.

"Try a few casts," I suggested. "Just to see how it feels."

Rebecca Sheffield was what you'd call a natural. Though her first few casts were stiff and awkward, she soon eased into the timing, placing the fly within inches of the targets I pointed out.

"You've had some casting instruction?" I asked her.

"A friend taught me," she answered. There was a long pause. "His dog used to sit behind me and catch my line when it dropped too low."

I'd pictured one of those yuppie casting clubs or a week at a flyfishing school. The idea of Rebecca casting into the grass with a dog minding her backcast hadn't entered my mind. I chuckled, and Rebecca turned to look at me.

"I still have the dog," she said. "Sometimes we practice."

I shoved off, and the boat drifted down the center channel. I aimed it at the shore and nodded at Rebecca.

"Go ahead. On the far side, as close to the willows as you can without hanging up."

Rebecca fired the fly just short of the willows.

"That shadow under the white stick up there: it's a fish," I told her. "Drop the fly in the fast water and let it drift over him." Rebecca's cast was right on the money, and he came for it. "That's you," I said. "Lift."

The fish was on. Rebecca kept her rod high, and mechanically reeled him in. I netted the fish with a triumphant swoop and held it up for her to see. Rebecca sat quite still. She looked surprised and mildly annoyed, as if catching a fish was something she had never really intended to do. She didn't show the slightest inclination to handle the fish. I dipped my hands in the water and removed the trout gently from the rubber mesh.

"Your first fish. Want a picture?" Rebecca shook her head. "Want to release him then?" Her back stiffened, and she turned away.

"You do it," she said.

Maybe nobody had floated this stretch of water in a long while. Maybe there'd been an invisible hatch or an imperceptible change in weather. I'd never seen so many fish in the water or so many brought to the boat. The wind tossed her fly into deep pockets. The willows spit her flies back at her. The fish were everywhere they were supposed to be, big fish. They came up for dragging flies and streaked out for short casts. The fish apparently loved Rebecca, in spite of her indifference. Or maybe that was her secret. Sometimes when people tried too hard, forced their hands, things had a way of not working out.

A client who was excited about catching fish on a day like that would have lost concentration, botched more casts, sent more flies into the willows. Someone whose heart pounded at the sight of a trout coming up for a fly with its big white mouth wide open would have involuntarily jerked that fly away. Not Rebecca.

She made her casts and carefully observed the fish as they came for the fly, setting only when the fish had turned with it.

Just after noon, we pulled in for lunch on a small island, beaching the raft in a backwater. I opened the cooler with some apprehension. If a dozen 18-inch fish before noon didn't impress her, I didn't figure she'd be too thrilled with a box lunch from a local greasy spoon. But if Rebecca minded the food, she didn't say so. She tried a little of everything and took the beer I offered her. She seemed to relax a bit, as if she preferred lounging on the grassy bank to the strain of fishing. We talked, and though she seemed reluctant to talk about herself, she showed an interest in the shop, the length of the season, and the other guides.

"Why do you do this?" she wanted to know.

Because if you do it long enough, it becomes more than just a challenge or a sport or even your job. Because the river seeps slowly into your life and washes away everything else. It slowly takes you over, until the only way to do it is to live it, to be on the river every day. I didn't think Rebecca was anywhere near understanding that.

"I'd rather be out here from May to September than stuck behind a desk all year, trying to find a few days to get away," I explained. That sounded kind of lame, but it seemed to satisfy her. She was quiet for awhile, and then she started in again with the questions.

"You seem so independent. How do you like working out of a shop?" she asked.

I shrugged. "Andy's a good guy to work for. He's fair with the guides, and I've got a chance of buying in."

She nodded, agreeing with the business end of it, I suppose. "The owner's ... wife," she said carefully, "does she fish?"

"Andy's not married," I replied. "Used to be, I hear, but he never talks about it." Except to say one night between bottles of tequila that he'd been a fool for running out on his wife. But that wasn't really any of Rebecca's business. "Don't know much about him really," I continued. "He's from back East, like you. He dropped out for a year or so a while back. Fished everywhere there is to fish and eventually ended up here."

I couldn't help wondering what Andy would think of Rebecca. The local girls didn't seem to interest him much, though they were all over him like flies. He wasn't a small town kind of guy. Rebecca wasn't my type. But she was a match for him, all right, New England accent and all. And she sure could fish, even though she didn't seem to get too excited about it.

Rebecca drew up her legs and rested her chin on her knees. She looked up the side channel where a small feeder spring, overgrown with wild cress, tumbled into the backwater.

"It's beautiful here," she said. Maybe there was hope for her yet.

"Finish your beer," I suggested, getting to my feet. "We'll walk around the island and nymph a couple big ones out of the fast water."

"You go," she said. "Take your rod. I'd just like to sit awhile." She took a charcoal drawing pencil from the inside pocket of her vest, tore open a paper lunch bag, and spread it flat on a stone. As I walked away, she began sketching the boat and, behind it, the river. I almost forgave her, about the fish, I mean.

I walked quickly around the island, where I took a pair of decent browns out of the side channel. The wind came up after a bit, and I figured it was time to get back to my client. I cut back through the willows rather than taking the long way around. It took me a minute to locate Rebecca. She was on her feet, at the edge of the backwater, fishing across to the opposite bank. I crouched in the willows, watching her strip in line and send out cast after cast. The wind was playing havoc with her line, and she was losing patience, dropping her backcast and muttering to herself when the casts fell short.

The fish that she was working lay across the slough, in a pocket two feet long and less than a foot deep. A tree branch had fallen across the mouth of the pocket, causing a small jam of sticks. The big brown hugged the backside of the pocket, surfacing occasionally to take an insect in the swirling foam. The fish lay so far under the willows, she'd have been hard-pressed to get a clean shot at it with a gun, let alone set a fly in front of it. I smiled. So that was it. Rebecca liked to play the long shot, the impossible fish. If only she'd told me at the beginning of the trip. I'd have put her onto some real tough customers.

It was an impossible cast, but somehow she

managed it. Her line lay across the branch, and the fly drifted back into the foam. The fish came, taking its time. The big brown opened its jaws. A huge half-circle of white closed on the fly, and Rebecca sucked in her breath. She set the hook as the fish turned. The line skidded down the length of the branch and miraculously came free. The monster felt the hook and bolted downstream. She didn't have a prayer of holding him if he got into the fast water. I stumbled out of the willows, hollering instructions.

"Follow him!" I yelled. "Run!" She ran, without a backward glance, racing the fish downstream. I splashed into the river beside her. She had good tension on the fish. He hadn't taken much line yet, but he would when he hit the fast water. I glanced at Rebecca. Her face was flushed, and her eyes were bright. She stared into the water intently, watching for any movement of the trout. The fish hit the current, and the reel screamed. Rebecca reached instinctively for the spinning reel. I anticipated her movement and grabbed her wrist.

"Do you want this fish?" I asked. She nodded. "Then let him run. He'll come back when he's ready. Just give him some room."

I released her wrist and looked down at her. She met my eyes, then raised her hand and deliberately jammed the reel. The line pulled straight, and the fish was gone. We stood there, in the river, glaring at each other. I seriously considered breaking the rod over her attractive head.

"I thought you really wanted that fish," I said finally.

"I did," she said. "But not on those terms."

She handed me her rod and walked back to the boat. I should have realized then that she wasn't talking about the stupid fish.

⌒

Considering the circumstances, Rebecca was remarkably pleasant for the remainder of the float. She said she'd had enough fishing for one day; she just needed some time to think. She settled back in the boat and demonstrated a quiet interest in the scenery and the wildlife. As we floated through the bends of the river, the tension in her face gradually faded. We checked Poindexter Slough on the way back, but I couldn't get her interested in wetting a line there. When I dropped her at the motel in the early afternoon, she insisted on paying for the whole day and tipped me generously. Still, I couldn't help feeling I'd let her down.

"Come back to the shop with me," I suggested. "You can meet Andy, and we'll go for a drink."

Rebecca frowned and shook her head. "I don't think Andrew ... Andy ... would appreciate that," she said softly.

There was something in the way she said his name. It took a little while for it to sink in. And then I understood that I was looking at my boss's former wife.

Well, that explained a lot of things, like why she'd broken off a brown that any flyfisher would have given his casting arm for and why Andy hadn't shown the slightest glimmer of interest in anyone else. But it raised a lot of new questions, too, like how much of all of this was up to me, the guide. But springing it on me like that, she didn't give me much time to think.

"You never know," I said. "Maybe he would. You took a chance coming all the way out here to see him. It's a long shot, but so was that fish back there."

Rebecca shook her head. "You were right," she said. "Andy's got to run. Maybe he'll come back when he's ready. Back home he was always saying that he needed more room. I thought it was me, but it isn't. It's this ... this Wild-West town, the fish, the willows, the canyons, the sage, that big, big sky. This is what he meant."

She opened the door and stepped out of the truck.

"Do you want me to tell him you're here?" I asked, knowing I would, regardless of her answer.

She slammed the pickup door and leaned back in the window. She pulled the ribbon from her hair and shook it loose. Her eyes were shining, and she smiled for the first time that day.

"Tomorrow," she said slyly. "When I'm gone. Just tell him I wanted to see what this crazy flyfishing thing was all about."

I figured if I timed it just right, Andy would be pounding down her door about the time those long legs of hers stepped out of the shower.

"Will do," I promised. "Anything else?"

"Just out of curiosity," she said. "How big do you suppose that brown was?"

Messing With the River Gods

EVERY SEASON FOR THE PAST 10 seasons, you have made a faithful pilgrimage to this river of rivers. In all the years you have visited these waters, you have taken away with you only the memories of a few special fish. You have left behind only your footprints and perhaps a few flies in the willows. In the company of other anglers, you have referred to this stretch of water only as the River X.

You figure your fishing karma on this particular river must be pretty good. So why in the name of all the river gods is the 10 o'clock trico hatch in full swing at 9:30 in the morning? And why is another fisherman standing in the middle of your favorite run with a good fish bending his rod and better fish rising all around him?

Under these circumstances, a lesser angler might rudely cut in upstream and muddy up the bottom of the river real good. But not you. Fortunately, or unfortunately depending on how you look at it, your fishing manners are impeccable. You'd no more cut in upstream than you'd go fishing with a can of worms and a jar of cheese balls. It's not that you're a fanatic about stream etiquette. It's just that it doesn't pay to mess with the river gods.

You step into the water at a respectful distance downstream and watch as the gentleman lands his fish. He raises the net, revealing the big forked tail and grayish mottled sides of what is obviously the most disgusting whitefish in three counties. A smile creeps over your face. Slowly everything begins to make perfect sense. After all, if the river gods have seen fit to place another angler in your favorite fishing spot and transform that spot into whitefish heaven, who are you to question their motives? Trusting entirely in their wisdom, you tie on a size 20 trico and calmly shake out a few feet of line.

Something catches your eye on the bottom of the stream. Through the swirling water, you can clearly make out a huge red-orange lure, all three of its barbaric hooks grinning up at you. Your forehead wrinkles in disgust. The river gods will not be pleased. You feel it is somehow your duty to remove the offending object from their domain. On the other hand, the water is waist-deep and spring-creek cold. You'll take a bath if you reach for it.

Just then, a few feet off the right riverbank, something very curious happens which suddenly demands your full attention. In smooth, flat water, all of 6 inches deep, a small boulder suddenly appears and behind it, a riffle that fans out 4 feet wide and 20 feet long. As you watch, the boulder disappears, reappears, and eats a trico. You dare to hope that the riffle is, in fact, a raft of feeding fish lying tail-to-snout in the wake of the monster at their head.

You fire a perfect cast at the head fish, cursing your stupidity the instant the fly hits the water. If you hook or even spook the lead fish, the others will scatter. You hold your mouth just right, and the fish ignores your fly. The fish behind him goes for it and misses. The fly slides over the back of another fish and into the upper jaw of the next fish down the line. You set the hook and the fish comes obediently downstream, silvery-pink sides flashing.

You decide to pick off the trout one by one, working through the 14-inchers at the back toward the monster at the front. You cast into the tail-end of the pack. A fish turns and pursues the fly downstream, nearly colliding with another fish that streaks over to snatch it away. You land this fish, another saucy rainbow, and release him.

Then it happens. The upstream fisherman reels in, clambers up the bank, and starts walking toward you. He takes his time, stopping every few feet to peer over the side of the undercut right riverbank. Panic-stricken, you gesture frantically, motioning the intruder away from the bank, away from your fish. The angler stops in his tracks, looking puzzled. Then he turns in the direction of your frenzied pointing and nods his head, finally comprehending.

"Grouse," he shouts, cupping his hands around his mouth so that the sound will carry even better. "A pair." And he keeps on coming.

For centuries, the rules of fishing etiquette have been modeled by esteemed mentors and publicized by concerned writers. Trouble is, there exists no effective means of enforcing them. If an angler chooses to walk downstream close to the bank, shouting, there is nothing to prevent him or her from doing so.

You find yourself wishing that every fishing vest came equipped with a hand grenade. No, not a hand grenade. That would be too noisy. What you really need is a bow and a single silent arrow, straight and true. Thwack. Toppling the intruder backwards. Away from the fish. You wonder whether the jurisdiction of the river gods extends above the high-water mark.

The riffle disappears, dark shapes streaking past you on every side, and with them your dark thoughts. The madness passes, and the gentle angler within you returns to inhabit your waders. You remind yourself that the creature on the bank is a human being, while the creatures in the water are, after all, only stupid fish.

"Howdy," says the human being, smiling and oblivious. "Catchinany?"

"A few," you say. "But it looks like it's all over now."

"What about later?" he asks. "Boys at the shop said this river's got a noon hatch of mayflies."

You nod in agreement. "Some stretches are better than others," you say thoughtfully. "There's a decent stretch about four miles upstream. Turnoff is just after the bridge. Can't miss it."

The two of you hike back to where your cars are parked, chatting amiably. You take down your rod and offer him a beer. You give him a half-dozen of the sparkle duns you tied in the wee hours of last night.

"What do I owe you for the flies?" he asks.

"Tell you what," you say. "The next time you're on your home river, just give away a few flies, and we'll call it even."

"I'll do that," he says. "People sure are friendly around here."

As his pickup heads off down the road, you give him the thumbs up sign. Then you string up your rod again, faster than you thought humanly possible. On the way back down the trail, you make a bargain with the river gods. If they bring back the riffle fish, you will take a swim in the icy river to retrieve the treble-hooked lure that is currently polluting their aquatic environment.

The river gods keep their end of the bargain. By the time you have hiked back down the trail, mayflies are popping all over the place, and the fish are back. You take 20 fish in 20 casts. The big rainbow goes four pounds easy.

You forget about your end of the bargain. Understandably, when you're having a day like the one you're having, you tend to get a little preoccupied. As you release the big trout and watch him swim away, you feel positively light-headed. You take a few steps toward the bank and trip over a boulder you're sure wasn't there this morning. As you go under, sputtering, you remember the lure. You mark its location with the toe of your boot, take a deep breath, and plunge into the icy water again and again. It's not that you're a fanatic about stream garbage. It's just that it doesn't pay to mess with the river gods.

Reading the Water

THE THREE OF US ARE HEADING for Helene Lake in Mike's pickup. Mike is driving and my son, Dylan, seated between us, is quietly checking him out. It was a new experience for Dylan, waking up this morning with a man in the house.

The logging road, usually closed to the public, has just been opened for the fall season, and the fishing is supposed to be excellent. I was happy to have this local information, this inside tip, this trademark of the serious angler, to pass on to Mike when he arrived last night. Mike is a Montana guide that I have known for a few months. In July I left Dylan with my parents and drove south across the border to Montana to fish. I was reluctant to leave Dylan like that, but he seemed secure enough with his grandparents. They insisted it would do me good to get a way for awhile on my own, and I suppose they were right. You have to start somewhere.

"Where do you live?" my son asks, and somehow his young voice carries above the noise of shifting gears and flying gravel. I'd prefer to take this road more slowly, watching for moose, and trying to preserve some of the stillness of the place. But Dylan seems to enjoy the four-wheeling, and Mike is obviously pushing it a little for Dylan's benefit.

"I live in a town called Dillon, in Montana," Mike shouts.

I realize he has to raise his volume over the racket, but I am startled by his loud, deep voice. At first I think he is annoyed with Dylan. For a split second, I am even frightened of him, but this is silly. Despite his size, Mike is one of the gentlest men I have ever met.

"Wouldn't it be funny," shrieks my son, "if my name was Dylan and I lived in a town called Dillon?"

I smile at Mike over Dylan's head, a little embarrassed. I have missed this obvious connection between the two of them and left the way wide open for Dylan to blurt out his question.

"Wouldn't it be even funnier," yells Mike, down-shifting, "if your mother's name was Paula, and she lived in Dillon, too?"

He hasn't slowed down in time for the curve, and the truck takes the corner in a skid. My right foot punches the floorboards, and I throw my arm across Dylan's chest to keep him from bumping his face on the dash. Dylan's eyes get wide, but he doesn't say anything. When we are safely through the skid, he reaches up and grabs Mike's cap, which he claps on his own head. They are both grinning like idiots.

At the lake, Dylan watches as Mike and I unlash the canoe and carry it down to the water. It's an old wooden canoe that Mike has restored, coating it with a clear layer of fiberglass instead of stretching a canvas over it. The thin strips of wood are visible from the outside as well as the inside. It is criminally heavy compared to the new synthetic boats, but considerably more stable in the water and very fast.

Lately I've been looking at canoes in sporting catalogs. There is a nice 16-foot Kevlar boat I think I could manage to get on and off the car by myself. In a year or two, Dylan will be big enough to help. I mentioned it to Mike last night, asking his advice, and he shot me a strange look.

Dylan is assigned the job of holding the rope so the canoe won't float away while we let Mike's dog out of the truck and unload the rest of the fishing gear. It is impossible for Dylan to stand still for very long, and he is soon leading the canoe around as if it were a pony at the end of a rope.

"Here Scout! Here boy!" he yells, slapping his side as Mike's dog jumps down from the truck. Scout's tail is going, and he can't decide what to do first. He runs in circles a bit, relieves himself, bolts down to the lake, and dives right in. He's a retriever.

"Mom, can we get a dog?" yells Dylan. I don't answer. We have been over this a hundred times. It would hardly be fair to leave an animal locked up in the house all day while Dylan is in school and I am at the office.

"He wants you to throw him a stick," says Mike, dumping a load of paddles and boat cushions on the bank. He beaches the canoe, and Dylan runs to find a stick. We watch to see where Dylan throws it.

"Good arm," says Mike, appraisingly.

"I play T-ball," says Dylan. "Jesse's dad drives us."

Dylan doesn't like me to come to his games. He says I make him nervous, but what he means is that I embarrass him. He says the other mothers stand around talking. They're not always whistling with their fingers and yelling, "Good arm, good arm!"

For some reason, I have assumed that Mike and Scout will go out in the canoe while Dylan and I fish the bank, like we always do. Scout is all ready to go, sitting in the bow of the canoe, dripping wet.

"Out," says Mike. Scout slinks reluctantly out of the boat and back up onto the bank. Mike reaches for a life jacket. It is a child's size, and it looks brand new.

"You sure you want to do this?" I ask. "He's never been in a canoe before."

"Mom, I'm not a baby," Dylan protests.

Mike shrugs and pulls the life jacket over Dylan's head. "What can happen?"

Plenty can happen. You don't protect a child simply by flipping a life jacket over his head.

"Sit still in the canoe and do what Mike tells you," I say, trying to strike a fair balance between concern and nagging.

Scout whines a bit as I give the canoe a good shove with my foot. I raise my camera to take a picture before they have gone very far from the shore. The two figures, pulling away from me in the wood-strip canoe, are in clear, sharp focus in the center of my lens.

When the canoe is out of sight, I find I have lost my initial enthusiasm for fishing. Scout and I poke around on the shore, exploring. We angle around a swampy area and discover a stream where kokanee are spawning. I count only 20 fish lying in the trickle of water that barely wets their backs. Usually I am intrigued by the sight of spawning fish, especially salmon. I am fascinated by their drive to perpetuate the species at such great cost to the individual fish. Today I find it disturbing, wasteful. The fish wiggle eagerly forward in the gravel until their bodies are only half-covered by the water, easy targets for bears and osprey. Scout edges forward and licks the back of one of the fish.

I head over to the far shore of the lake, which has recently been logged. It is rough going through the slash, and my walking stirs up clouds of black flies which have somehow survived the first killing frosts of the year. The sun is shining brightly now, as it does in late fall. The hills behind the lake are brilliant, almost luminous with yellow aspen. This gives the impression that a fire is raging on the opposite shore, but the ground and the slight wind off the lake are cool reminders of the true season.

The sun has warmed the water enough to stir the bugs into activity. There are a few coming off the water now, a few fish rising. I wade in among the submerged, charred stumps and begin casting. I catch and release several healthy fish, some kokanee and a few which must be hatchery trout. The sun is quite warm now. I am just about to get out of the lake and remove my jacket when I see the canoe coming back into view. Dylan is kneeling in the front, executing some very splashy paddling. Mike is paddling on the opposite side with deep, slow strokes that propel the canoe forward in a series of long, fast glides. I step back up on the bank, whistle for Scout, and start slowly back, figuring I will meet them just as they come off the water.

Mike's rod is still strung, propped up in the corner of the canoe and extending over the side. The fly has come loose from the flykeeper and is bouncing along on the water behind them. The canoe is less than 50 yards from shore when a fish streaks across the surface after the trailing fly.

I raise my camera and start shooting. Mike will be surprised to find that I have captured this fish on film. The rod bends, clatters, flips and goes over the side. Mike lunges for the rod, and the canoe goes over. Unable to look away, I am still taking pictures.

The overturned canoe. Mike standing chest-deep in the water. Dylan surfacing in his life jacket. Dylan splashing. Mike reaching for the rod. Mike hauling Dylan out of the water by the back of his life jacket. Plunking him back into the canoe.

The camera's automatic advance shuts down when the film runs out. By the time I reach the boat-launch site, Dylan is screaming.

"Shut up. It's only water," says Mike. This is a new voice, cold as the mountain lake.

"Leave him alone," I say.

I pick Dylan up and carry him to the truck, where I

dry him off and help him change into the set of clothes I always bring along just in case something like this happens. As soon as he is dry and dressed, Dylan hops out of the truck and runs over to where Mike is dragging big piles of brush onto the road. I remove the roll of film I have just shot from my camera and sit in the back of the truck, wondering why I was stupid enough to entrust Dylan to this huge stranger.

You entrusted yourself to this stranger. That very first day and that very first night.

There is a difference between entrusting yourself and entrusting your child.

When I get out of the truck, I find that Mike and Dylan have got a big fire going, a huge fire. Even though it is high noon and the sun is beating down, even though we have brought sandwiches for lunch instead of hot dogs, they have built this huge fire. Mike has dragged some stumps over. We sit on those and stare into the blaze.

Dylan takes a bag of cookies from the cooler. He steps across Mike's feet and comes to sit in my lap. I help him open the cookies. He takes one out and hands it to me. Dylan takes a cookie for himself, carefully separating the two halves.

"Mike saved my life," he announces solemnly. "Didn't he, Mom?" He twists in my lap and looks straight into my face for confirmation.

Dylan adores him. There is a connection between them already. There are some things that you just can't do for him.

Dylan is not old enough to think for himself. I make the decisions for the both of us.

Mike pours me a cup of coffee, which I refuse.

"Paula," he says. "He wasn't in any danger."

"Yes, he was," I say.

"He had a life jacket on. He was swimming."

"That's not what I meant. You reached for the rod first."

"If you thought he was in danger, what the hell were you doing taking pictures?"

"I don't want to talk about it."

I finger the roll of film in my pocket. It is the only chance I have to hold on to my anger.

It was an accident, the canoe going over. It is a small thing, reaching for the rod first.

My friends say I'm too cautious. If a man loves you, he will love your son like his own. I don't know about that. Dylan's father disappeared on us. This sort of thing happens all the time. There are laws for recovering the money part of it. There are never any guarantees, but there are little signs, I suppose. Odd, uneasy little feelings that don't fit with the other feelings we are having, instincts we suppress until it's all over and we look back with the clarity of hindsight. Looking back, the warnings were always there. Dylan's father used to go off by himself.

It's a bit like reading the water. That day we met, on the river, Mike helped me cross a bad-looking stretch. He took my arm and guided me through the fast water over the slippery stones. Halfway across, he stopped, pulling me closer on his downstream side, shielding me from the current. Then he pointed out the landmarks on the far shore, showing me how to read the water ahead of us. He taught me to distinguish the ripples on the surface that were the swirls of rising fish from the ripples that were rocks beneath the surface.

Mike tosses another pile of brush onto the blaze. He comes to sit beside me and takes my hand. It hangs limply in his, neither resisting nor responding.

"Paula," he says gently. "What exactly am I doing here?"

I make an effort now to picture the three of us together, living in Montana, but I cannot hold the image together long enough to even get us through the drive back to town. Everything is happening too fast. If I were brave, I would tell him the truth. I would tell him that I need more time. That a year from now I will probably find the canoe story hilarious, that now I am grasping at straws for a reason to push him away. That most likely it has nothing to do with him at all. That I am very lonely. That I am afraid of making another mistake, though more for Dylan's sake than for my own. That I no longer know which feelings to trust and which to deny. That I am just not ready.

"I need to know," Mike says.

"We are fishing. Reading the water."

Mike tips his head back. When he looks at me again, his expression is wary, focused. He walks down to the lake, brings backs the child-sized life jacket and props it up near the fire to dry.

"I think the Kevlar boat would be ideal for you and Dylan," he says. "But I think you already knew that."

I take the film out of my pocket and toss it in Mike's direction. He catches it with that easy, aggravating way men have of catching things one-handed. He waits until the last second, hand forward, wrist loose. Then his hand snaps back, and he snags the film in midair.

The Spent Fish Conversation

A SERIES OF PARALLEL CHANNELS guided the migrating salmon up the first hundred yards of the Fulton River. Beyond this maze of man-made channels the fish had schooled in a shallow concrete holding pond. Except for the slow fanning of their gills and tails, the fish lay suspended, immobile in the aspic-thin glaze of water which barely covered and separated them. Their red-orange backs were a shade darker than the salmon pieces I had seen drying on wooden racks at the Indians' fish camp on Babine Lake.

The migration of the salmon signaled the end of summer and the completion of my work at the archeological site near Old Fort Babine. After two months of communal tenting, I sympathized with the close-packed fish, wondering how they could manage to breathe in the crowded pool. At the same time I could barely resist an odd temptation to cross the river on the fishes' exposed red backs which were strung out over the water like a miniature boom of cedar logs. I pictured myself falling through, the boom of log-like fish closing silently over my head. The Indians believed that when natural creatures returned to their own communities, they appeared as humans to each other. I wondered what I would look like to the salmon people falling into their underwater village from the sky.

Further upstream the salmon disappeared swiftly and singly into the current, and I followed the vanishing fish up the river like a roe-hungry trout. When the thick willows made the riverbank impassable, I halted on a stretch of water about 40-feet wide where the moderate current spread over a coarse gravel riverbed. I fitted the sections of my graphite rod together and attached an old Hardy Marquis. Stripping a few feet of line I winced at the angry-Merganser grate of the reel. I threaded the sink-tip line through the rod's guides and tied on a roe imitation.

Wading cautiously into the river I shook out the leader and loaded the rod with several awkward false casts before setting the line across the river. I moved slowly downstream, methodically covering the water and trying to keep my backcast out of the willows. I missed several good fish before deciding to strike at the slightest hesitation in my line, even if it meant hauling the heavy sink-tip out of the water prematurely.

Several drifts later I hooked a decent fish. It took off downstream, the Hardy's shriek sawing into the silence. A few yards into the backing the fish seemed suddenly to tire, and I tentatively began to bring it in. At the first sign of resistance from me the fish broke water, thrashing menacingly. It was no trout but a large salmon, foul-hooked just above the tail.

I had difficulty controlling the snagged fish on my light rod. A full 20 minutes later the fish lay exhausted in the shallows. I normally released the fish I caught, but there was no sense in trying to revive the spent salmon. I dispatched it with a quick blow to the head and bent a willow branch through its gills in order to carry it more easily.

I had covered a fair bit of river in the past hour, and the sun was beginning to set. Gripping my rod in one hand and the fish in my other, I clambered up the riverbank intending to walk back along the gravel road that fisheries vehicles used to maintain the dam farther upstream. I walked as quickly as I could, but it was difficult to carry the big fish whose tail dragged in the gravel. The salmon was bleeding slightly and gave off a strong fish smell.

Just as I began to worry about attracting a bear, there was a commotion in the bush ahead. Steeling myself for a confrontation with a grizzly, I felt terribly relieved and a little silly as two young native boys tumbled out onto the road roughhousing and laughing. When the boys saw me they marched right over, pointed at the fish, and laughed even louder.

"Hadi'," I said solemnly, greeting the boys in dialect. The boys stopped laughing instantly and exchanged a quick glance. They looked thoughtfully at my neoprene chest-waders, dismantled flyrod, and the orange roe imitations drying on my vest.

"Howdy," said the taller boy. After a long pause he added, "Nice fish."

During the boy's pause I interrupted, "Are you from here?" Then in answer to his comment I added, "Snagged this fish by accident."

At precisely the same time the shorter boy said, "Once we caught a whole sackful of trout."

I felt bad about killing the salmon and was not in the mood to swap fish stories. "This is not a trout. It's a salmon," I explained wearily and unnecessarily.

To which the other boy replied, "Warden got us though."

"Comes by here every night about this time," continued his friend.

I made a show of putting down my gear and the salmon. "So, do you boys live around here?" I asked.

"And the warden, he took all the fish," the tall one answered.

The conversation kept floating up on its side like a spent fish unable to right itself in the current.

The villagers were accustomed to speaking indirectly when making polite requests. Maybe the boys were hinting that they wanted my fish. I offered it to them.

"No way!" they exclaimed together and began laughing again. The sound of a vehicle coming up the road silenced them. The tall boy quickly scooped up the salmon, and both boys disappeared into the bush.

I was still standing, confused, in the middle of the road when the green fisheries truck pulled up.

"Nice evening for fishing. No luck, eh?"

I shook my head. "Couldn't find a trout. Snagged a

salmon though. Had a devil of a time landing him on my fly rod."

"I'll bet," he laughed. "No harm done. Won't live much longer anyway. Good thing you released him."

"What do you mean?" I asked cautiously.

"Regulations are a bit confusing around here," explained the fisheries officer. "You can keep the land-locked salmon you catch in the lake, but the sea-run salmon coming into the river are protected."

The spent-fish conversation suddenly righted itself, held steady in the current for a moment, and disappeared into the night.

The fisheries officer checked my license and continued down the road. As soon as he was out of sight, the boys stepped out of the woods.

"Thank you," I said. "The warden told me that this is an illegal fish. I think you were trying to tell me that, too."

I hesitated to ask the boys what to do with the fish. Clearly, it could not be wasted. The coastal peoples had elaborate rituals for returning parts of harvested fish to the river, even their ashes, in order to perpetuate the run. I did not know the local customs.

The boys exchanged a few sentences in dialect that I couldn't follow.

"The bears come to the river at night to eat the salmon," said the tall boy. I nodded.

The three of us walked down to the river, and I laid the salmon in the shallows of a back eddy where it could not drift away. The water flowed gently over the riffles, lapping at an occasional boulder and overturning small rocks with a muffled underwater knocking. I looked upstream and wished the salmon a safe return to the village of his people.

Rattlers

On YOUR WAY TO FISH this hot new place you've been hearing about, a place of big fish and few people, you run over a snake that's trying to cross the road. You stop the car and assess the damage through the rearview mirror. Looks like maybe you clipped the snake just behind the head with the left tire and just ahead of the tail with the right one. This happens in the shadow of an outcropping called Rattlesnake Bluff. Chances are it's a rattler, but you'll never know for sure unless you actually see the rattles, because there are also bull snakes around that have the same coloring and the same diamond-shaped markings.

I sympathize with your predicament. I've been in a similar situation before, trying to determine whether the snake I'd just seen my 3-year-old whack with his toy shovel was a rattler or not.

"What did it look like?" I'd asked him as calmly as I could manage, peeling off his play clothes with shaking hands, looking for marks.

"Well, first it looked like an S," he said. "Then it made itself into a Q and made the S-noise." Sesame

Street will do that to a kid.

There's only one way to settle this thing. Just hop out of your car and go have a look. Then again, the snake might still be alive and not in the best mood, having just been run over by a vehicle.

You put the car in gear and drive on. You haven't gone a hundred yards when you start thinking how much fun it'll be walking into the shop in the morning with a set of rattles tucked under your leather hat band instead of the wimpy little mallard feather you've got there now. You put the car in reverse because there's no room to turn around on a road like this, and you back down the hill you've just come up until you reach the spot where you think you hit the snake. Only it's really hard to tell just exactly where that is now, mostly because the snake is gone, and there were no skid marks to begin with.

      ☞   ☞   ☞

WHEN YOU TOLD THEM where you were headed that day, the boys at the shop exchanged a look that prompted you to ask if there was a problem, like maybe the Beaverhead suddenly dried up in just that one spot or the rancher whose property you have to cross finally got mad and drilled someone between the eyes.

"Nothin' like that," they assured you. "It's just the guides have been killin' rattlesnakes there pretty regular the past few weeks." They don't mean to put you off this spot entirely; it's worth the risk if you're up to it, but they do recommend if you're hiking in a ways to stay up on the frontage road as long as you can where the snakes are a little easier to see.

As you walk along, every rattler story you ever heard starts playing in your head. Like the one about the fellow riding in Garden of the Gods who got bit when he stepped off his horse too close to a pile of sagebrush and almost bit it because he insisted on being driven to the military hospital 30 minutes away where his medical coverage was good instead of the public hospital just 20 minutes away. Of course, by then you're a good half hour into your hike, and you still haven't quite run out of stories. There's this good one you heard Tim telling, and you can't quite recall how it went, but you've just run out of road because this is where the trail cuts off to the really good spot.

You make your way down the trail, tapping the high grass in front of you with your rod and stomping your feet down heavily as you go, sending plenty of warning vibrations ahead. If you see the rancher with the gun coming, you'll walk right over and turn yourself in instead of ducking down in the grass like you usually do. You've already given up on ever reaching the river alive, so when you finally stumble out of the brush and onto the bank, it comes as a wonderful surprise. Since there's no need to begin adopting a careless attitude at this point, you wade right into the water, waist deep, just to be safe, and start stringing up your rod.

You've got the line through the guides, and you're

concentrating on attaching the fly when, out of the corner of your eye, you see something coming down the river. It's a rattlesnake, no doubt about it. It swims right up to you, kind of puts on the brakes for an instant, turns its head to one side and looks at you before it bolts across the river and up the trail you just came down. You tell yourself you weren't really in any danger, because a snake can't strike unless it's coiled. Still, you figure it would have given you a bit of a start if the snake had mistaken your dark brown neoprenes for a nice rock or branch to climb out and rest on. That's when the shaking starts, and, like it or not, you've got to make your way back to the bank and sit down for awhile.

"What's a bloody rattlesnake doing in the water anyway?" you ask yourself, and while you're pondering that, you remember Tim's story. It's the one about the time on the Big Hole when a snake came up the oar, and a quick-thinking client grabbed something, beat off the snake, and saved the guide from having to make a choice between entertaining a snake in the boat or rowing the rest of the trip with just one oar.

⌒ ⌒ ⌒

THE GUIDE HAS JUST MANEUVERED the raft into a long bend of the Missouri River, a place where the rocks of a railroad bed angles down steeply into the water.

"Nothing but hogs in here," he says. "Get ready."

On his advice, you cast very tight to the bank, and

you spot several fish ahead. The guide starts rowing with the current. Up on the railroad tracks, three figures are coming toward you, and you hope you reach the fish before they walk by and put them down. As the boat drifts within range, you make a cast that your no-nonsense guide pronounces "good enough" to get you a fish, and you are concentrating hard on your fly when you hear a young voice.

"Hey, dad! There's a rattler! I'm gonna get him!"

The boy, seven or eight years old at the most, picks up a big rock and walks off, presumably in the direction of the snake. The two men just stand there on the tracks, finishing their conversation, and waiting for the boy to finish the snake.

Somewhere in the distance, you hear the voice of the guide.

"That's you."

"Hit him!"

"Set the goddamn hook!"

Conditioned as you are to respond to that word, you set the hook immediately on a nice brown. He makes a run, you see to it that you have tension, and you even allow yourself a quick glimpse of the fish before your attention reverts to the tracks.

The boy hoists the rock over his head and hurls it to the ground. If he runs away at this point, you might land the fish, but the boy is bent over in the tall grass, and you lose sight of him. That's when you stand up in the raft, losing your balance and the fish.

You don't know what becomes of the child, because

you drift past him. But you know you will get nightmares about it, the guide chewing you out for losing that fish, I mean.

⌒   ⌒   ⌒

YOU'RE IN THE HIGH DESERT on a pack trip with your son; riding, fishing, showing him what living out West is all about. There are several other fishermen along, and there's a woman, too. She happens to be the guide. Somehow a little rivalry gets going, maybe because you're there with your son, whatever. You don't know how it got started, but it's there.

She senses it too. Maybe that's why you're on the gelding that hasn't quite got it straight yet that he's a gelding while everybody else is on a nice, quiet mare. But that's OK with you, because you've spent a few seasons on a working ranch, and you figure you can hold your own on a trail ride, not like most dudes who wouldn't know a left lead from a right lead if it came up and bit them on the ass. You can be sure the rest of them didn't saddle their own horse this morning like you did. Not that you'd want to get into anything resembling amateur rodeo with her, though. She'd probably have an edge on you there.

Just wait until tomorrow, though, when the fishing starts. She doesn't look like the fishing type. The leather case she's got strapped to her saddle most definitely looks a gun and not a fishing rod. All right. Maybe she can fish, but she probably doesn't flyfish. Flyfishers don't carry tackle boxes.

Then the horses start acting a little edgy. They're prancing, and the ears are going all directions like they're trying to locate a sound out there in all that sage.

"Stay here," she says to the rest of the group, but she motions with her head for you to ride on up ahead with her. You walk the horses up another 20 feet before you spot the snake, coiled at the base of a juniper. She dismounts, leaving her reins in place across the horse's neck. She takes the lead rope in her hand, lets it fly, and whacks the snake in the head with the metal piece at the end. Kills it dead. She picks up the snake, still coiled, and looks around for a place to stash it, but her saddlebags are full, and your horse is more than a little nervous about the smell of snake. She takes off her hat, crams the snake inside it, and puts it back on her head. She carries it that way all the way back to camp, where she skins it and cooks it up for dinner.

That's it. She wins, and the fishing hasn't even started. The way you see it, a woman like that can fish any damn way she wants.

Reading the Water

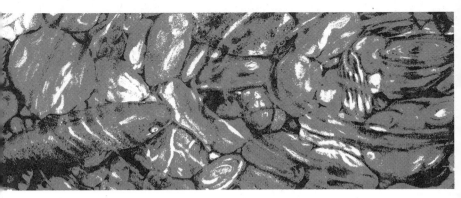

Part II

Eddies & Seams

Of course, waiting out there in the dark with the sky full of bats and owls, we sometimes begin asking the great questions that can kill time so nicely: sex, death, and fly-fishing; the meanings of life and sport: are we real participants or just observers, and what kind of difference does it make?

— John Gierach
Sex, Death, and Flyfishing

Reading the Water

The Virtual Angler

BUDDY BAILEY STEPPED INTO the outfitting kiosk and keyed the six options he always selected whenever he intended to fish the Yellowstone: three-millimeter neoprene waders, stream cleats, a 12-pocket vest, a 9-foot-6-inch graphite rod, a Hardy reel, and a weight-forward-6-weight line. Moments later, the boy exited the booth, a walking fiche of ancient angling history.

Zaak Walton, Chronicler of Sportfishing Antiquities, inclined his head in amusement at the sight of the emerging figure and lifted his hands in a gesture of surrender. "All right," he said, "but this is absolutely the last time." He took an HMD from the rack and set the helmet upon the young man's head. "It's probably a mistake to indulge you, my boy," he said. "These old games are irreplaceable. But I dearly love to watch you fish. It's like seeing one of those ancient angling videocassettes come to life. Quite ancestral for me, now that I think about it."

The boy stepped into the wade pool, selected a freestone bottom, and increased the water volume to 8,000 cubic feet per second.

Zaak frowned. "That's pretty heavy water," he called. "Sure you want it that extreme?" Buddy glanced at the water beginning to bubble up around him, grinned and nodded. Zaak turned to the game console. "Activating rod," he announced.

Buddy held the rod close to his side, raised his arm, and began moving the rod slowly back and forth, 10 o'clock and 2 o'clock, establishing a rhythm. A thin beam of light shot up the length of the rod, leveling out at its tip, and extending in length with each movement of the rod.

"Looks good," shouted Zaak. "Ready?"

"Ready," answered the boy.

"WELCOME TO THE YELLOWSTONE," said the Gillie's synthesized voice.

Buddy turned his head to the left and, downstream, the yellow rhyolite cliffs of the canyon came rapidly into focus. He turned his head sharply to the right, experiencing a moment of dizziness as his gaze shot over the tumbling water to register the change of scene. From the observation platform above, Zaak saw the boy stumble momentarily in the churning pool and then regain his footing.

Buddy scanned the river in front of him, focusing on a large boulder across and slightly downstream. "Query trout," he requested.

"AFFIRMATIVE," came the reply.

"Show me," said Buddy.

Top and side views of the cutthroat flashed in rapid succession across the scanner. A schematic of the fish's location plotted its holding space 6 centimeters behind and 17 centimeters right of rock center. Buddy felt something twist, fish-like, inside him. Just a picture, he reminded himself. He gripped his rod more tightly.

"Proceed," instructed the boy.

"SELECT FLY. FOR HINT, USE QUERY MODE."

Buddy's hand moved automatically to the simulated sheepskin patch on his vest, and he tapped the third synthetic fly from the left.

"ROYAL WULFF, SIZE 10. CAST OR MOVE ON."

Zaak watched as Buddy raised the rod and lengthened the laser line with a series of false casts. It was a pity that the old-style games had no spectator effects, and, yet, there was no question in Zaak's mind that Buddy had located a fish. The boy's stance had changed. He was tense and alert. Buddy's arm punched forward, and the beam hovered just above the boiling surface of the wave pool, angling downstream.

"GOOD CAST. DRIFT AVERAGE."

Buddy made a circling motion with the rod and the beam curved into a loop and jumped a short distance upstream.

"FULL MEND. DRIFT UPGRADED."

Buddy's arm shot up, and the beam angled straight down to the water.

"FISH ON. TIGHT LINE."

Inside the helmet, the reel sounded in Buddy's ears, and he smiled to himself as he recalled his ancestor's words. *My reel sang today with the music of a most extraordinary fish.* The old one was a bit poetic for my taste, but he was right about the English reels, Buddy thought. They have the best effects. The duration of the sound and its high-pitched whine suggested a good fish, a sensation confirmed by the increasing torque on the rod.

"INTO THE BACKING. ADVISE DRAG."

In response, Buddy palmed the reel. Eventually the fish slowed.

"END RUN."

Buddy reeled in the cutthroat. Three icons blinked before him on the screen.

"WEIGH, HOLOGRAPH OR TERMINATE."

Buddy held the rod to one side and reached into the water. I may not get another chance after today, he thought. What had the old one said? *Though it almost cost me the fish to bring him so quickly to net, I wanted to spare the creature. As a result, the fish required no reviving, and I barely had time to remove the hook and admire his exquisite coloring before he flicked his tail and disappeared into the river.* How odd to release a fish. But odder still to kill a fish when violence was so clearly forbidden in all other games.

"WEIGH, HOLOGRAPH OR TERMINATE. PLEASE ADVISE."

"Release fish," said Buddy. Zaak leaned over the rail.

"FISH RELEASE STRICTLY PROHIBITED BY FEDERAL REGULATION 1126B PURSUANT TO

THE ANIMAL RIGHTS ACT OF THE YEAR 2020."

Buddy stretched his arms out and quickly lowered them into the water. *I had held the fish for the briefest instant, but the heft of him will remain a part of my angling memory forever.* My god, how he envied the old ones. What would it be like to hold a fish, another living creature, and return it to the water?

"ILLEGAL ACT. AUTHORITIES NOTIFIED. SYSTEM SHUTTING DOWN."

Zaak put his head in his hands. Where had the boy gotten the idea of releasing a fish? All references to catch-and-release fishing had been carefully expunged from the virtual angling program. The boy tore off the helmet and clambered out of the pool. "What now?" he asked.

"You heard the Gillie. It's illegal to release fish. The virtual angling games are hooked up directly to the Wildlife Division. Unfortunately, you've been reported."

"It's a game!"

"Gamers are subject to the same ethics restrictions as citizens are. You know that."

"Yes, sir," said the boy. He looked down at the floor in an attempt to conceal his excitement. After he had released the fish, before the program had shut down, he had seen the fish swim away. The original program must have contained a loop for fish release. The old one was correct. They did release their fish.

"Fortunately you have an impressive record of

terminations to this date — 180 fish last week alone. I think I can get you out of it with some counseling, but you'd better let me handle it. Go home."

Zaak turned back to the terminal and initiated the program re-build. Buddy entered the outfitting kiosk, dissolved his gear, and keyed his home designation. Zaak frowned and bent over the monitor.

"Damn!" he said. "We've lost the program."

Following the protocol designed to avoid the embarrassment of a directed visit, Zaak Walton issued an official invitation to his superior, and moments later, Dory Roosevelt, Senior Wildlife Manager, occupied Zaak's visitation chair. She entered the briefing mode and was acquainted instantly with the details of the incident.

"I see," she said. "Would you recommend the boy's exclusion from the virtual angling program then?"

"I am gravely disappointed in the boy's behavior, of course, but I would hate to lose him. He's our most promising prospect. Last week, for example, he had a perfect score on *Beaverhead*, Streamer Level, and a 50-fish day on *Henry's Fork*."

The manager cleared her throat and looked Zaak directly in the eye. "Nobody has a 50-fish day on *Henry's Fork*," she said.

"Buddy did. Midge Level. And half of his fish were over 20 inches."

"I see," she said. That explained Zaak's protective attitude towards the boy. Still, it might be better to separate the pair of them for the next phase of the program. "Well, if the boy is that good, why isn't he involved in something that at least has decent graphics. *Firehole*, for instance. Why does he waste his time on a primitive archival program like *Yellowstone*? It's second-generation reality at best."

"The young man has a sentimental and perhaps a genetic attachment. His ancestors fished extensively in the park. In fact, releasing the fish may have been triggered by some ancestral impulse."

"Is counseling your recommendation then?" she proceeded.

"Yes, and public hours to be carried out under my supervision."

"But he has destroyed an irreplaceable program."

"Not in its entirety. I've managed to recover the technical aspects of the game, the equipment functions and the fishing parameters. The scenery is retrievable from the archives. Only the fish are lost. Oddly enough, they are missing from the backups, too."

Ms. Roosevelt made a note to order a trace on the artificial intelligence component. Perhaps it was developing some ideas of its own on the subject of fishing. "Surely we have other cutthroat sequences," she said.

"Yes, but the Yellowstone cutts are distinctive. The substitution would not hold up to the scrutiny of an authentication panel."

"I remind you that we have a responsibility to the citizenry to preserve Yellowstone Archival Park exactly as it was passed down to us."

"I am fully aware of our responsibilities," said Zaak. He hesitated. "That's why I want to take Buddy into the park with me to reproduce the game. That would give him an opportunity to make full restitution."

The woman rose from her chair and leaned over Zaak's console. Behind her gold-rimmed optics, her eyes flashed. "Out of the question! The Purists would have our heads. The park has been closed to the general citizenry for more than a century. I might consider letting you go, but that boy's a minor. The park is crawling with life forms, and there's no climate control out there. The insurance liability would be outrageous."

"Frankly, Ms. Roosevelt, he's the only one who can do it."

"Oh, really, Mr. Walton. And were you not genetically selected, enhanced and educated to know everything there is to know about fishing from the publication of your esteemed ancestor's book in 1653 right up to the end of outdoor angling in 2093?"

"I was, indeed, and it is widely known that my ancestor wrote an early book on fishing. But with all due respect, may I point out that the first book on flyfishing was written by Dame Juliana Berners, circa 1421. I hesitate to confess this to you, Ms. Roosevelt, but my ancestor was a bait fisherman, and the flyfishing sections in his treatise were written by a friend."

The Purists insisted on the smallest possible production crew. They were adamant that the party be teletransported directly to the site, avoiding the thermal areas, and the expedition's insurers were quick to agree. The animal rights people took a hard line at first but eventually agreed to a strict limit of 10 replacement fish, taken from the same locations as in the original production. They also granted a permit for the filming of any wildlife that wandered accidentally into the scenery, reminding the petitioners that the park's animals had already endured centuries of hunting, fishing, species-inappropriate feeding, disruption of habitat, photographing, bird-watching, and other appalling invasions of privacy under the protection of the so-called conservationists. Zaak produced a photograph from the park's collection showing a primitive conveyance with its doors peeled completely away by *Ursus horribilis*, and the expedition was reluctantly granted permission to carry a tranquilizing gun to be used only in the most dire emergency. To no one's surprise, Ms. Roosevelt volunteered to take charge of the gun and, somewhat apologetically, produced the genetic credentials necessary for large-weapon handling. In the end, the expedition consisted of Ms. Roosevelt, Zaak Walton, Buddy Bailey and a production crew of three.

❦

Buddy joined the others at the park's symbolic gate at 1400 hours, wearing a colorful hover-boarder jacket and helmet in addition to the regulation park uniform he had been issued. "My mother insisted," he shrugged, entering the pre-transporting inspection area. He indicated his parent, who stood smiling nervously and waving from the adjacent security paddock.

"We specified forest-green," said the Purist representative.

"It's not such a bad idea," interrupted the expedition's insurance agent. "Those jackets are rated for falls at speeds of up to a hundred kilometers per hour. Besides, it'll look bad if we override a parent's specifications and there's a claim."

"Empty your pockets," demanded the Purist.

"He's a teenager," said Zaak. "Ten to one, he's got food in there."

Buddy reached into his pocket and, grinning, produced a handful of Mars bars. "Imported," he said. Then he reached into another pocket and extracted a small book.

"I'm bringing this, too." It was a reproduction of a fishing journal. "Family archives," he said. "This one's about the park. Can you read without a converter?"

He handed the journal to the Head Chronicler, and Zaak turned a few pages reverently. Ms. Roosevelt passed her hand over the entry post and keyed in the coordinates Zaak had given her. The symbolic gate opened.

"Are you going to stand there reading, or do you want to go fishing?" she asked.

The Purist blanched.

"Bream me up, Scottie," said Zaak, and the group members entered the transporting cubicle in single file.

They were conveyed instantaneously to their destination. Buddy recognized the landscape at once. All around, the yellow lava cliffs of the canyon rose up sharply from the water's edge. Across and slightly downstream, a large boulder emerged from the churning water. Though Buddy had imagined the scene over and over again, had scoured his ancestor's journal for descriptions of the landscape, he was unprepared for the reality of it. Without the restriction of a visor, the sky was too vast, the sun too bright, the cliffs too sheer. Buddy cupped his hands around his eyes as if to eliminate the overwhelming intensity of detail. Unlike the wade pool, the water was not uniformly, circularly, activated. He studied its surface. In places, the water ran straight and swift; in others it curled back upon itself. There were soft-looking high places behind the rocks which fell off into frothy riffles. The river stretched out before him, with width and breadth, flowing from one direction to another. Yes, the journal was correct. If you gave up your footing, the river would rapidly carry you from one place to another. He tossed a stick into the water, and watched the river quickly sweep it away. The reality of what he was about to do struck him with the full force of the river. He turned to Zaak. "Thank you for this," he said, "whatever happens."

"You'll be fine," Zaak said.

"No way," said Ms. Roosevelt.

"Give me a reading on the water volume," Zaak said to the parameters technician.

The man aimed a remote at the river. "Four thousand cubic feet per second," he answered.

"Too risky," said Ms. Roosevelt.

"He can handle it," said Zaak. "He was wading eight thousand when he blew up the game. Get into your waders," he said to Buddy, "and don't forget the stream cleats. Ms. Roosevelt," he said, "if you have concerns about our safety, perhaps you could direct them more constructively toward the creature up there."

The Senior Wildlife Manager pivoted and scanned the cliff above. The large cat's tawny coat blended in completely with the overhanging ledge, and its location was not immediately apparent. When she saw the creature, Ms. Roosevelt reached silently for the tranquilizing gun.

"Look at the claws on that thing," she said. "Maybe we should have gone to Buffalo Ford. Bison may have horns, but at least they're not carnivorous."

"If we don't have any luck here, we may have to go to Buffalo Ford," said Zaak.

The crew had finished taking its readings. "We're ready to go when you are!" the director yelled. The manager looked nervously at the cat, which lifted its head at the sound of the human's voice and then went back to licking its paws.

Buddy had finished suiting up and was busily rigging a graphite rod. Zaak chose a size 10 Royal Wulff from the box of synthetics and carried it over to him. "I'd rather use this one," said the boy. He opened his fist and Zaak picked up the fly.

"Peacock herl, calf tail and elk hair," he said. "Those are restricted materials. Where did you get this?"

Buddy shrugged.

"Don't let Roosevelt get her hands on it," said Zaak. "Do you know how to tie it on?"

Buddy rolled his eyes, knotted on the fly and stepped into the water. Dear god, he thought, I am standing in the river. I am going fishing. Perhaps the old one stood where I am standing now. Yes, he must be here with me. The boy waded carefully into position across from the boulder. "Query fish?" he hollered over the sound of the water.

"Better be," breathed Zaak. "Activate rod!" he called.

Buddy held the rod close to his side, raised his arm, and began moving the rod slowly back and forth, 10 o'clock and 2 o'clock, establishing a rhythm. Then he began to strip handfuls of line from the reel. The line shot up through the guides, and the length of his backcast grew. He set the line down on the water, well ahead of the boulder, mending upstream with a quick flip of his wrist. The fly drifted into and around the boulder, bumping against its water-smoothed surface. A large cutthroat rose without hesitation from behind the boulder, turned and took the fly down with him.

"Fish on!" yelled Buddy. The fish ran, and Buddy palmed the reel. He followed the fish a short distance downstream and netted him in a quiet backwater. He had been warned not to handle the fish, but he turned the net from side to side in the water, marveling at the fish's golden color and bright slash of red on and below the gill cover. With great reluctance, he passed the net to the parameters technician, who had been hurriedly trained to humanely dispatch the cutt and seal it in a black plastic tote.

"We got it all," said the director. "Let's do it again."

They were in the middle of the tenth sequence when the storm moved in. The shooting had run well into the late afternoon, and they had mistaken the slow darkening of the sky for the setting of the sun. If anything, the disappearance of the sun had been connected with a noticeable improvement in the fishing, and Buddy was standing, midstream, playing a fish, when the crew found themselves suddenly pelted in a freezing rain. The sudden downpour of sleet was followed almost immediately by a flash of blue light and a tumultuous roar.

"What is it?" yelled the director.

"Lightning!" shouted Zaak. "Electrical disturbance!"

"Will it interfere with the lasers?"

"Don't think so!"

"We'll finish up then! This is the last fish, and I'd like to get these effects on ROM. Okay, Ms. Roosevelt?"

The manager signaled her approval, and the members on the bank struggled into their waterproofs. The light and the noise were unpleasant, but there was no immediate danger. Still, it was her responsibility. "Just stay within the 50-meter radius!" she cautioned.

"If anything happens, I'll E-vac us out of here, and I don't want anybody left behind. Do you hear me?"

The director nodded and turned back to his console. The technician elevated him to his previous position above the water. The director's platform was suddenly outlined in blue. A ball of lightning rolled down the extension arm and across the surface of the water. In the flash of light, Zaak saw Buddy turn and submerge himself in the water, holding the rod high above his head. The current swept him away.

"Buddy!" Zaak staggered to the undercut riverbank and disappeared over the edge.

Ms. Roosevelt fumbled for her transmitter and pressed the E-vac button. They were back in the transporting cubicle; herself, the parameters technician, the film technician, and the director, badly burned. She vomited.

The storm had abated as quickly as it had arisen, and the sun had reappeared, though its evening rays were short-lived. They had drifted clear of the canyon and into a grassland plain where the river widened and flowed more gently. Buddy removed his helmet and spread his jacket on the bank. With a pocket-blade, he slit the outer sleeve and extracted a packet from the compartment where the elbow-protection disc should have been. He set the packet on the ground some 10 meters away, punctured the seal, and stepped back. The shelter inflated and leveled itself. The site was perfect. Buddy slit the other sleeve and retrieved a sleepsac.

"Just one," he said. "We'll have to stick to the lower elevations. Sorry about that, Mr. Walton, but I never figured you'd want to come, too."

He glanced at Zaak, sitting beside him on the riverbank. The old man hadn't spoken yet, but he would come around once the shock reversal took hold. Buddy made a sweeping motion in the air and held his clenched fist in front of Zaak's face. He opened the hand slowly, revealing a small brownish insect, its tent-like wings folded over its body.

"Caddis," he said. "Not many yet, but in another half hour I figure we'll have ourselves a pretty decent hatch."

The boy picked up the jacket and emptied the pockets. He dropped the fishing journal into Zaak's lap and carried the nutritional and medical supplies over to the shelter. The sun went off the water. Buddy rigged the rod and tied on an elk hair fly. The fish began to show themselves.

"The way I see it, Mr. Walton, between us we know just about everything there is to know about fishing. I'll bet there's not a fish in the park that we can't catch. That journal there is full of stories about the good old days when there was plenty of fish to go around and big ones, too. I figure a hundred years is long enough to bring a river back, don't you?"

Zaak rose to his knees. Clouds of caddis flies swarmed on the banks, and fish slashed noisily across the surface of the water. Zaak nodded his head.

"Welcome to the Yellowstone, Mr. Walton," said Buddy. He took the man's arm and helped him rise to his feet. "Are you gonna be all right? We can't stay here long, you know. This is the first place they'll look."

"I'll be just fine after a bit," said Zaak. He let go of Buddy's arm and took a few tentative steps on his own. "As the Compleat Angler himself pointed out, Providence has a way of watching over us fisherfolk. Now quit your yakking, my boy. Be quiet! Be quiet; and go a-anglin'."

Reading the Water

Droppers

You're being ungrateful and you know it. Your guide is busting his ass. It's 100 degrees in the canyon, the heat only partially alleviated by a stiff upstream breeze, and the water is running high. Nevertheless, your guide has held the boat back to allow you second and even third chances at missed fish. He has rowed into the shallows and dropped the anchor every time you hooked a decent fish. He has netted your trout, removed your hooks, repaired your leader and dressed your flies. He has identified every life form which has crossed your path this morning by its correct Latin name, and just as the Latin was becoming a bit highbrow for your tastes, he launched into a series of fetchers regarding the gang of outlaws who used to hole up in the canyon area.

It's lunchtime, and you have just wolfed down the last of the marinated kebobs which your guide has grilled to perfection streamside. He has graciously offered you the remaining imported beer, even though you suspect it is his personal favorite, and even though you would be just as happy with one of the dozen bargain brands still on ice. He is doing everything right. There is only one problem. After a year of planning and saving for this trip, after a 40-fish morning, and following the perfect lunch, you have realized that what you want most on this earth is to catch just one blessed fish all by yourself.

You will have to get rid of the guide. Not permanently, of course. Just temporarily, while you catch your trout. You have already picked out the fish. The trout, which you spotted as the boat pulled in for lunch, is lying in the shadow of a rock a mere 20 yards upstream. He has risen exactly seven times since noon.

Your guide opens the imported beer and hands it to you. "Forty fish," he says. "That's not a bad start."

"Thanks to you." You raise the bottle in a one-sided toast. "I'll bet you have 40-fish days all the time."

"My clients ... " he begins.

"Not your clients. You. I'll bet you have 40-fish days all the time."

A strange, searching look passes over his face. For the first time today, your estimable guide has drawn a complete blank. "To tell the truth," he confesses, "I can't recall the last time I actually went fishing." He shakes his head sadly. "Maybe I need a break."

"Now that you mention it, so do I," you say. "I'm all fished out for the moment. Think I'll just stretch out here in the shade for a while."

Your guide is crestfallen. "The PMD's should be starting up here pretty soon," he says. "There's a nice bit of pocket-water downstream I thought you'd like to wade."

"Well, you'd better grab your rod then and get down there. I'll come looking for you in a bit." You stretch out on the rocks, and the guide frowns. "Go on, git," you say. Eventually he gits, but before he departs he sees that you are comfortably settled on a self-inflating thermo-rest pad with boat cushions for pillows, your rain gear and a roll of toilet paper just an arm's length away.

"Watch out for the poison ivy," are your guide's thoughtful, departing words.

The instant he is out of sight, you dash to the boat. You grab your rod, inspecting the leader, the size 10 Royal Wulff and the small trailing ant. That tiny ant has been, in fact, the only real source of friction between you and the guide all morning.

"I don't like to fish droppers," you protested.

"Trailers," he said. "The second fly is attached to the bend in the hook of the lead fly using a clinch knot rather than the traditional blood knot arrangement used on droppers."

"Oh," you say. "Well, I find that it's twice as hard to get a float, I always end up watching the wrong fly, I wreck twice as many leaders, it feels like cheating, and eventually I forget I'm fishing two flies and run one into my hand."

"No problem," said the guide. "I know this nifty way of removing hooks. You wrap a piece of monofilament around the bend, push the eye down, tell the victim to count to three and pull on two. Besides, you'll catch twice as many fish."

At the time, it seemed pointless to argue. But now, carried away on the wings of your new independence, you grab your nippers and sever the ant, sticking it on the guide's fly-patch for safe-keeping. You goop the Wulff and prepare to stalk your fish.

As you make your approach, you watch the fish. The big brown is lying below a rock, protected from the full force of the current, his long shape casting a shadow on the sand beneath him. He holds, motionless, moving a few inches to take something underwater or to inspect a particle on the surface. You measure your casting distance this side of the rock, and when you have it right, you let the Wulff fall just slightly ahead of the rock.

The brown rises on the first cast. He swims toward the fly and knocks it with his nose. Somehow you manage to leave the fly on the water. For a heart-stopping six feet, he follows the fly downstream, bumping it once again before returning to his lie below the rock.

"No," you say as the truth settles in. *He would have taken the ant.* You head for the boat to rest the wary fish and retrieve the severed ant.

There is something different about the boat. It is further from shore than you recall, and the anchor rope, which was hanging loosely from the pulley, is now stretched taut. But you are in no mood for distractions. You clamber into the bow, locate the ant, and attach it to the Wulff. As you trim the knot, you hear the unmistakable sound of wood scraping over rocks, and it dawns on you that the boat is moving. You spring into the rowing seat, and the guide's voice comes to you, echoing the advice he delivered as he negotiated Deadman's Rapids earlier that day.

"Nothing to it. Just point the nose of the boat toward the danger and row away from it."

You row, or try to row. There is obviously enough water to move the boat, but there is not enough to dip the oars into. Yet. The right oar hits a rock and pops out of the oar-lock, bruising your chin. You leap into the water, retrieve the oar, and dig in your heels to the extent that river sandals permit digging in. You grab the boat, and it glides past, bruising your shins. The pain is slightly reduced by the numbing effect of the 53-degree water. You wince, but you don't let go, and the boat comes around. You ease it into a back eddy and wedge the anchor behind a rock, piling further rocks upon it in the style of those markers you find along the paths in certain parts of England. As you sit down to examine your shins and contemplate the near-disaster, the big brown rises again. This time you are ready for him.

You wade carefully upstream, positioning yourself straight across from and slightly downstream of the rock. You execute your cast with precision, a backhand cast thrown with enough slack to ensure that the ant will precede the Wulff downstream. The cast is right on the money, and the ant drifts toward the fish's lie. The fish moves two feet out of his feeding lane and gobbles the Wulff. You set the hook, amazing yourself and the fish. There are a few tense moments when he wraps your line around the rock. You free the snagged line with a gentle roll cast and net the fish after his second run. As you move to unhook him, the fish writhes in the net, throwing the fly. You reach for the leader and run the Wulff into the heel of your hand. You release the fish, a lovely blur of gold and red, owing to the tears in your eyes. You and the guide arrive back at the boat simultaneously.

"Back so soon?" you ask.

"I noticed the water coming up fast, and I got a little worried about the boat. Thanks for moving it. Nice cairn," he adds, indicating your rock pile.

"Any luck?"

"I was a bit too early. The mayflies are just starting to come off, so I came back to get you."

You nod and hold out your hand. "Damn droppers," you say.

"Trailers," he says. "Not to worry. I've got this secret way of removing hooks."

"I know," you remind him. "You told me about it. But it won't work on me, because I know about the counting to three and pulling on two."

He shrugs, wraps a length of monofilament around the bend, and pushes the eye down.

"Count to seven then," he says, "and I'll choose a new number."

"One," you say, and the hook's out.

He washes the wound with peroxide and applies a Band-Aid. He pops the Wulff into a plastic box, labels it with the name of the river and the date and hands it to you.

"Souvenir," he says. "Anything else exciting happen while I was gone?"

"I caught a fish," you say. When the guide glances at your bruised shins, you add, "He put up a real good fight."

"Where?" the guide wants to know.

"Upstream. Below a rock."

"Which rock?"

You point out the rock, a smooth red slab sloping into the clear green water.

"Big brown?" he asks. "Red spots, small scar between the adipose fin and the tail?"

"The very one," you say. You look him straight in the eye. "That ant sure is one great dropper."

For the second time today, your guide looks bewildered.

"Which ant did he take?" he asks slowly. "The brown or the black?"

"The black," you say.

The guide scratches his head. "Funny," he says, "I've never heard of that fish taking anything but the Wulff."

Reading the Water

Mentors

My FATHER CARRIED MY SUITCASE up the stone steps. I followed with my aluminum rod tubes. He watched as I set them carefully in a corner of the screened-in porch. If he thought it was strange that I'd taken up fishing again after all these years, he didn't say so.

I stepped into the cabin and looked around. The first thing I noticed was the down parka I'd sent my father for Christmas. It was hanging in the closet, with the brand tags still on it.

"Something wrong with the parka?" I asked.

Dad set down my suitcase and kicked the heavy pine door shut. "Waste of money," he said. "Don't need a coat."

I forgot all the promises I'd made myself about not starting anything.

"This is bloody Ontario. Forty degrees below zero in December. What do you mean, you don't need a coat?"

"When it gets real cold, I wear three shirts."

Three shirts: long johns, a wool Pendleton, and a plaid McKenzie over that. No gloves, except when he would head for the woodpile. And yet, I remember, any time he took my hand, his were always warm. No hat, either, as I recall. A fishing guide without a hat was a genuine oddity. Every Christmas a grateful client would inevitably send him a cap which he would toss onto the top shelf of the closet. For all I knew, the hat collection was still there, gathering dust.

I'd forgotten how rugged he was, much tougher than the tourists he took out fishing for muskies and northerns. He'd scoff at their high-tech reels, their many-pocketed fishing vests and fingerless fishing mitts. A down parka had tourist written all over it. God only knows what he'd think when he got a look at my fly rods.

I was beginning to have second thoughts about bringing them at all. This was lake country, big lake country, where they fished down deep with 30-pound test and live bait. The tackle stores sold steel leaders and lures like pan-sized trout. You couldn't walk into a shop and find the times of the hatches and the river conditions neatly chalked up on a bulletin board. With a fly rod, you were on your own.

Dad struck a match, turned up the gas on the propane light, and lit the mantle. "You know where everything is," he said. "I'll see you in the morning. We'll go fishing if you want." He nodded in the direction of my aluminum tubes.

"Sounds good," I said.

⌒

When I was a very small girl, I used to go fishing

with my father. Sometimes we took the boat. Often, we walked from our place at the 7-mile railroad bridge to the 9-mile bridge, a long walk for a child. My arms always ached from carrying the minnow bucket, but I wouldn't have dared complain and risk being left behind on the next trip. My father took his fishing very seriously and tended to be a bit gruff with anyone who wasn't tough enough or didn't fish properly. I always wondered whether he was that demanding with the fishermen he guided. Occasionally I'd put the minnow bucket down to pick wild strawberries or to rescue a mud turtle that had fallen over onto its back while attempting to cross the tracks. As I walked, I filled my pockets with dew-bright pebbles, which later faded to a disappointing gray.

At the 9-mile, I was content to sit in one spot, dangling a line over the side while my father paced up and down the bridge, trolling a line in the swift current. When I grew tired of fishing, I'd lie face down on the ties, watching for fish in the shadow-striped water below. The fish were long, dark shapes in the water, sending sprays of shiners to the surface ahead of them.

"You're not catching anything," my father would say when he came to check on me. "Get a fresh minnow."

The hook went in the minnow's mouth, out through the gills, and back through the tail, missing the internal organs. That way, the minnow stayed alive for some time on the hook. Occasionally I think of those open-mouthed, gasping minnows when I am tying on a fly.

When I am releasing a fish, I think of the buckets of fish entrails we hauled to the dump. My father would scoop the tourists' walleyes out of the live well and clean them expertly and quickly. The filets were always piled neatly on the corner of the table before the discarded fish hearts had stopped beating. He used to show them to me, holding the pulsing hearts up on the edge of his knife before tossing the guts into the garbage pails. I stopped fishing when I was 15.

I learned what little I know about flyfishing from books. The literature is full of stories about fishing mentors, those pipe-smoking, tweedy types who provide the initiate with gear and skill and fishing etiquette. I used to think that my mentors were those unknown anglers I first observed on the rivers of British Columbia or the guides who took me out on my first few trips. The truth is, my mentors were gasping minnows, pails of fish waste and pumping fish hearts balanced on the edge of a knife blade.

⌒

I slept soundly. The first noise I heard was the sputtering of a boat motor. I rushed down to the dock in my housecoat, so I wouldn't be left behind.

"Daylight in the swamp," I murmured as I stumbled onto the float.

"Been daylight for a couple hours," Dad replied. "Too bad you missed breakfast. The motor was acting up, or you would've missed fishing too."

"I'll be ready in a minute," I said. "Don't leave without me."

It took a few minutes to get into my clothes, run a comb through my hair, and grab my gear.

"Since when are you so keen on going fishing?" Dad asked as we pushed away from the dock.

"Since I found out how civilized it can be."

"What's that supposed to mean?"

I fitted the sections of my fly rod together and attached the reel. "Flyfishing," I said. "It's different."

My father hooted and slapped his leg theatrically. "Well I'll be damned," he said. "Old Man Campbell used to do it."

"What?"

"Reggie Campbell, the guy I bought this place from," he said. "He used to flyfish. Tied all his own flies with fur and feathers from the game he shot. Crazy old coot used to hold the flies in his mouth while he tied them."

"You're kidding. Was he a good fisherman?"

"People thought he was awful strange to fish like that around here, but he did all right. He used to catch these big silvery-looking fish that nobody else ever seemed to catch. The Indians get the odd one in their nets. We used to smoke 'em."

I'd seen a picture of Reginald Campbell in the public library in Fort Frances. He wore a tweed cap and smoked a pipe. Suddenly I felt very optimistic. We rounded the point, and Dad cut the motor.

"We'll paddle up the channel," he said. "The fish are pretty spooky in here. Mind you don't drop anything in the boat."

I rigged my rod and tied on a streamer. Dad looked critically at the set-up.

"Be a real shame if a big northern smashed up that pretty little rod," he said.

"It's strong enough," I countered. "Graphite."

"What pencils are made of?"

I nodded. We quit talking then. Dad let the boat drift, and I concentrated on pitching the streamer against the bank, stripping it back in toward the boat and re-casting. It was difficult hauling the heavy sinking line out of the water, and my casting was a little shaky. My father wasn't fishing. He was hunkered down in the back of the boat. He had set a fleece-lined cap on his head and was busy pulling the flaps down over his ears.

"Since when do you wear a hat?" I asked him.

"Since my daughter got civilized," he answered.

"Don't worry," I said. "I'll watch my backcast. If it makes you feel any better, the hook's barbless."

"Barbless!" my father snorted. "Bass gets ahold of it, he'll shake it for sure."

A bit later, a bass did get hold of the fly. The fish dived under the boat and came flying out of the water on the opposite side. The bass shook its head viciously and spat out the streamer, which hit the side of the boat hard enough to break the hook point. I had two more bass on briefly, and a couple of takes from unseen fish that seemed to simply bite through the leader.

"I'm not much for fishing wet flies," I admitted. "I like fishing mayflies when they're hatching off the water. Fish flies, we used to call them. Remember how they'd be all over the window screens in the morning?"

"Still are," my father said.

I looked around the boat and spotted a large mayfly on a boat cushion, white wings folded together above its curved, tan body. I picked it up to get a better look, and the forked tails twitched.

"Reggie was always doing that," my father said. "Picking bugs up off the water and staring at them."

⌒

Just before noon, Dad finally pulled out his spinning rod.

"We gotta eat," he said.

A big walleye took the diver on the first cast. I turned my head as my father snapped the fish's neck.

I spent the rest of the day reading and puttering around in the garden, trying to restore the flower beds. Toward evening I set up my fly-tying materials and started working on a mayfly imitation that would match the one I'd seen that morning. Just after the sun went down, my father came up to the cabin and rapped sharply on the window.

"The bugs you were talking about," he said. "There's a bunch on the water down by the dock. Some fish, too."

I grabbed my rod and a couple of the new flies. It was a hatch all right, with large white mayflies coming off the water in good numbers. The pod of fish, splashy risers, was feeding on the surface. I tied on an imitation and cast it into the middle of the rising fish. I could barely see the fly despite its light color, and I lost track of it among the naturals.

"That's you," my father said suddenly. "Set him."

I hate it when they do that. Guides must be born with a special kind of radar. What did he know about flyfishing anyway?

I lifted the rod tip and struck the fish. It didn't run like a northern or tug like a walleye. It didn't dive or jump like a bass. It took a bit of line and thrashed around lamely, more like a whitefish than anything else. I glanced back at the pod of feeding fish, the splashy rises, the silvery backs, the big-forked tails. Surely there weren't any bloody whitefish in the lake. I let the line go a little slack, hoping to shake it off.

"What's the matter with you!" my father yelled. "Keep tension on him."

He grabbed the landing net and scooped up the fish. It lay flopping on the dock, its small mouth opening and closing. Before I could make any excuses, my father let out an ear-splitting whoop of astonishment.

"It's one of Old Man Campbell's fish!" he hollered. "The big silver smoking fish! I haven't seen one in years!"

The departure of their cousin didn't faze the remainder of the whitefish. They continued to feed noisily on the surface, creating riffles as far as the eye could see in the otherwise glass-calm bay. I could hardly claim that they were an endangered species, and as my father said, we had to eat. Still, if he'd put the fish in the live well, I might have sneaked down in the middle of the night and tossed the sorry-looking thing back. But my father didn't wait until morning. He hauled the smoker out right then and there, mosquitoes notwithstanding, and fired it up. Then he got on the radio phone, and by midnight everyone from the Seine River to Rainy Lake had heard the story of how his daughter from British Columbia had caught the big silver smoking fish on her flimsy little fly rod with a bug she made out of string and turkey feathers.

"By the way," he said to me between radio calls. "There's a bunch of Reggie's stuff out in the boathouse somewhere. The rods are only made of wood, but they're yours if you want them."

Reginald Campbell's lines had disintegrated, and the reels had seized up, but his collection of bamboo fly rods, carefully stored in metal tubes was in perfect condition. They are much too valuable to fish on a regular basis, but once a year I take one along when I visit my father up the lake to fish for Old Man Campbell's big silver smoking fish.

Reading the Water

The Facts

I GOT NO IDEA WHY he went along with it. Maybe all he wanted was the goddamn hat. Roddy, he comes down the ramp with this big old black plastic box hanging out both sides of the wheelbarrow, gotta be 4-foot square at least, and he's wanting me to hook it up, complete with a bloody pump, so it's got fresh seawater circulatin' through it at all times. Like we got room for this thing on a 35-foot gillnetter.

"What would you like me to throw overboard first?" I ask him. "The nets or the dinghy?"

Roddy just dumps the whole shebang over on the float, says we got no choice if we want to continue to fish in Area 4. Fisheries made it a condition of licensing last year that all the boats in the river got to have these things aboard, these live tanks they're called, to put the steelhead in. It's part of this catch-and-release program they got cooked up where the commercial fishermen are supposed to tag and release the fish. We ain't even after the steelhead. We're fishing the sockeye run that time of year, and the steelies just have the misfortune of being in the wrong place at the wrong time. Companies won't buy 'em anymore, so we don't like seein' them in our nets, but we got no way of keepin' them out either.

Anyway, they've got special hats for the guys that deliver live fish to the steelhead barge upriver. They've even got this $1,000 prize to be split between the commercial fisherman that tags the fish and the sportfisherman that catches it. Fisheries, the sporties, the processors, the Indians, they're all in bed together on this one.

Still, Roddy's the boss, so I hook the live tank up just to humor him, and it works like a charm right from the start.

"Good enough," says Roddy, which I figure is his way of saying that it's one thing to have the tank aboard and another to use it.

"Just don't get any ideas about me performin' mouth-to-mouth on any damn steelhead," I say, just to let him know that I'm with him on this.

"I'm sure it won't come to that," he says, but it bloody well came close.

Not a week later. Picture this. It's 20 minutes into the first opening of the year, five maybe 600 boats out there all jockeying for position, trying to get their nets into the water without runnin' over anybody else's. It's not a pleasant day, either, though it's sunny. You know how it can be in the river when the wind's blowin' one way and the tide's runnin' the other. Still, Roddy's got the situation all scoped out. Six o'clock on the dot, he's got the boat right where he wants her, and we're gettin' our nets in the water on the double. Couple of boats must of jumped the gun by maybe a minute or two, 'cause we see the Fisheries guys go by top speed in their Zodiacs. We no sooner made our set, nice sweep of line, corks all floatin' good, bloody water taxi comes chuggin' up to Roddy's boat with two dozen sportfishermen aboard, wants to put an observer on his boat, and Roddy says okay, just like that without so much as a glance at me.

They give him a choice of who he wants, and he picks the girl. He's got a daughter about the same age himself, college girl, so I figure he's doing it for the girl's protection. I mean, she'll be safe enough with the two of us, but there are boats where she'd have her hands full. Course the sporties don't know us from Adam, and when Roddy picks the girl, they start lookin' around at each other like maybe it's finally dawned on them that this might not be such a good idea. But the girl appears to have her head on straight. Right away, she pipes up, "No, I'll go." So her boyfriend gives her a peck on the cheek and hands her over which is not exactly a piece of cake given the four-foot swell, and he hollers that they're just going to find placements for the others and then they'll be back to pick her up.

Roddy looks at me, and I'm thinkin' what he's thinkin'. It's coming up seven p.m. already, which gives them four hours of daylight at most, providing the fog holds off, and the logistics of this thing just don't add up. How they think they're gonna place 24 people on different boats and collect them all before dark is beyond me. We got ourselves an overnight guest, though she don't know it yet. That's okay, because Roddy and I will be up most the night anyway, and she can have the bunk all to herself. In any case, she don't look like she'll eat much. She's past green, more like gray, and the front of her jacket looks like maybe she's even past the puking stage.

"Sure you got no qualms about comin' aboard with two old dogs like us?" I ask her.

"At least you speak English," she says. "The first six boats we hailed were Vietnamese. They didn't seem to know about the Observer Program."

"Never heard of it myself," says Roddy. "Anyway, I've got nothing against the Vietnamese. They fish hard. I respect them."

The girl looked at him. "I didn't mean anything by that," she said. "I was just stating a fact."

Then it's my turn to look at Roddy, who I grew up with. Over the last two days, suddenly he's been transformed into the champion of wild steelhead, women's lib and multiculturalism. And I wonder what's goin' on, but now we got company, and it's not the time to sort it out.

The girl's name is Jennifer, and she's from Telkwa, up the line. She's not gonna bother us. All she's gonna do is stay out of the way and record the numbers and species of fish that we take aboard. They're trying to get a handle on the number of steelhead taken as a bycatch. Turns out she goes to the same school that

Roddy's daughter goes to, University of Victoria, but they don't know each other. Jennifer is studying biology, and Roddy's girl is in commerce.

So we're all standing around having a chat like we're at a goddamn cocktail party instead of in the middle of the Skeena River making our first set on the first opening of the year, when Jennifer suddenly asks us how long we usually leave the nets out before we check them. By then, the cork floats are bobbin' up and down, signaling there's fish, and Roddy figures it's time to haul them in. We stand on either side of the stern, and Roddy winches in the nets. Nice sockeye, still wiggling, comes toward us. I grab the fish, whop it on the head, and toss it Jennifer's way.

"There's your first steelhead," I say.

Jennifer picks up the fish. "Blue back, v-tail, no spots," she says. "Looks like a sockeye to me. Male, five-year fish, seven pounds, ought to bring you $15 if you can deliver it in good condition." Roddy laughed like hell.

Girl stayed out of the way, I'll give her that. We finished pickin' that set without a steelhead. She seemed disappointed.

"How many steelhead do you think we catch anyway?" Roddy asked her. "Usually I go a whole season, only get three or four."

I think she was surprised at that, but then she looked around at the fleet, and she said, "Three or four fish and five hundred boats could add up to a couple thousand steelhead."

"And a couple million sockeye and pinks," said Roddy. "It's a drop in the bucket. You're trying to shut us down for a handful of steelhead."

"There are only a handful left," she said. "Anyway, we're not trying to shut you down, just relocate the boats out of the river gap slough at least, so fewer steelhead will be intercepted."

"Same thing," he said. "See any luxury yachts out there? A lot of these tubs wouldn't even be safe on the outside. Who says there's a problem anyway?"

"The test fishery at Tyee," she said. "The steelhead runs have been declining steadily. We're at half of the 10-year average this year and last."

"Something's haywire at Tyee," said Roddy. "Last year we had a poor return at Tyee, and sportfishermen on China Bar were catching steelhead like crazy. How do you figure that?"

"I don't know," she said slowly. "Maybe it was the weather. The surface temperature was way up. Maybe the fish just went down deep."

I damn near fell overboard. Gettin' a sportie to admit that maybe the Fisheries numbers needed some work, well, that was something you didn't hear every day. "Now what would your boyfriend say if he heard you talkin' like that?" I asked.

"It doesn't matter what he'd say," she answered. "I'm quite capable of sorting out the facts for myself."

Then I started readin' her loud and clear 'cause the way I figure it, there's basically two types of people in this world, people who believe in the facts and people who believe in loyalty. I'm a loyalty man myself, union all the way. Roddy gets himself in trouble, I wouldn't think twice about backin' him up, no matter what he done. And I wouldn't be squeamish about adjusting "the facts" either if it would help him out. And that's just the way it is all up and down the line. We got fishermen loyal to fishermen, processors loyal to processors, sporties loyal to sporties, and Indians loyal to Indians. Everybody lookin' out for their own interests and presenting their version of the truth to suit their own particular view of things. And out in left field, here, we got this one little pip squeak girl who thinks she's gonna sort out "the facts" and make up her own mind about what's goin' on like it's gonna make one damn bit of difference. I figure what she needs is one big dose of reality.

"So how'd a kid like you get mixed up in this?" I ask her.

"Because I flyfish," she says, "and because I'm a conservationist. I don't want to see one of the last runs of wild steelhead wiped out by a heavily subsidized industry."

"A lot of commercial guys sportfish, too," I tell her. "Went upcountry myself a year ago this fall. I see this guy fishing from a lawn chair. Hauls in a big fat coho, drops it heavy-like on the bank, and a big gush of eggs spill out. Then he whacks it on the head, and I say to myself, *They're killin' the mamas.* So don't give me any of your conservation horsefeathers."

"There are different kinds of sportfishers," she says.

"The people I fish with release all the fish they catch."

"Lay off," says Roddy, because he's got a pretty fair idea what I'm gonna say about that.

Second set we get a steelhead, and it's in pretty sorry shape, one eye missing and the gill cover torn. It's not even moving, but Roddy throws it in the live tank anyway just like he's supposed to, although we both know the fish is a candidate for the freezer and he's only doin' it to humor the girl. Jennifer rolls up her sleeves and gets right to work on the fish, holdin' it by the tail and swishin' it back and forth in the tank, forcing water through its gills. We don't tell her there's no point, because the fog is startin' to roll in, it's obvious that the water taxi won't be back tonight, and maybe it's better if she's got something to keep her busy.

Roddy filets a sockeye, then packs it in brown sugar and soy sauce and barbecues it right out there in the open. He takes a piece over to Jennifer, but she's too pre-occupied with the fish or maybe she still feels queasy, 'cause she says no thank you. She just sits there tending the fish and finally she falls asleep sittin' up, with her hand still trailin' in the tank. Roddy goes over, real gentle like, wakes her up and says she'll be more comfortable in the bunk below, and then he notices that the fish is moving around.

"Well, I'll be damned," he says, and we all gather around, starin' at the fish like it's some bloody miracle, but you have to admit that those steelies are pretty tough little customers after all.

Jennifer wants to stay up and keep an eye on the fish, but she's shivering by then and Roddy don't want her goin' hypothermic on us, so he tells her to go get some sleep and we'll babysit the damn fish. So Jennifer goes to bed, and Roddy and I stay up all night fishing. And every once in a while, he says to me, "We better go check on Jake." 'Cause by then, somehow, the fish has gotten nicknamed One-Eyed Jake after the pirate.

In the morning Jennifer is doin' much better in the sea-sick department. She gets up and looks at the fish, goes back below and fixes coffee and eggs and toast all around and even takes a couple bites herself. Roddy says if she'll learn to mend nets, he'll be happy to get rid of me and take her on as crew instead. She laughs and says she can learn to mend the nets, but she'll probably never learn to swear as good as me.

Later in the morning, we radio the Trauma Unit, which is what our guys are startin' to call the steelhead barge, and make arrangements to have the steelhead picked up. Young fellow comes out in this metal skiff looks like it was made of scrap but built real good, and damned if he ain't got a woman with him, too. Roddy looks worried when he sees the guy comin' in a metal skiff 'cause Roddy's boat is made of fiberglass, and he ain't too crazy about the idea of gettin' rammed, but the guy knows what he's doin'. He keeps his distance, and the woman throws over this big black plastic bag she wants us to put the fish in. This thing is long and thin with a zipper running down its length and mesh at both ends, real scientific looking except for this piece of frayed rope they got trailing from one end.

Jennifer unzips the bag, floats it in the tank, stuffs the fish in it, and zips it back up. Then I pick up the bag and carry it over to the side, and Jennifer follows, holding onto the rope so it don't tangle in anything. The woman on the skiff holds out her arms, and I toss the fish over to her, only Jennifer ain't ready, and she don't let go of the rope quick enough. The boat lurches, and the fish goes in the water, black bag and all. I'll never forget the expression on their faces: my skipper and both women glaring at me like I just committed murder on a baby. I guess that's why I done it. I jumped overboard. Risked my bloody neck to save that stupid fish.

Roddy and I got into that catch-and-release thing for awhile. A lot of our guys did. You'd hear 'em on channel 19, all excited about some fish they'd revived. Roddy and I had five steelhead in all in our nets, and we delivered three of those to the barge. One died on us, and the other we tagged and released ourselves. We figured we were doin' our bit. No way are we goin' to weedlines, though.

Things are going along just fine 'til the first of August, when Fisheries panics 'cause there's not enough steelhead comin' through at Tyee, and they shut us down in the river. Well, you never saw nothing like it. The fishermen go on the rampage. They got the Fisheries building in Rupert wrapped up in nets so nobody can get in or out. They got people marching up and down Second Avenue blocking traffic and handing out leaflets. There's a big sign sayin' honk if you support the commercial fisherman, and even at night, when everybody's gone home, people are still driving by and leaning on the horn. That's the kind of support we had.

Wasn't much to do while we were waiting for Fisheries to decide what they were going to do next. Some of the guys headed back south right away, out of disgust with the whole situation, but Roddy and I decided to hang on to the bitter end, hoping they'd open again, and we'd clean up with all the other boats gone. We ate real regular and worked on the boat. We even had time to catch up on our laundry and get our mail.

We got a postcard from that observer girl Jennifer, thanking us for having her aboard and for showing her another side of things; how, for guys like us, giving up our boats must be like giving up the family farm. She'd heard they'd shut us down and hoped we'd had a good season up until then. She said there were rumors that the government was about to allocate big money to count the fish properly on the Skeena. She planned to look up Roddy's daughter at school and wanted her address. She meant well, I suppose. Still, it bothered me, her writing like that. Most times it's just easier, cleaner, not knowing anybody on the other side. Probably for her, too.

Our last night in Rupert, Roddy and I sat at the galley table with a bottle of Canadian between us, just pouring and sipping, not talking much. The missing steelhead had shown up, a week late, but the fishery was over. Roddy made the decision to go south in the morning. Then he headed for his bunk, and the last thing he says to me is, "Kill 'em all. Kill every bloody steelhead you get your hands on." Which is fine by me.

Fishing With the Boys

Two hundred years before Izaak Walton penned *The Compleat Angler,* Dame Juliana Berners, a fifteenth century nun and sportswoman, published *The Treatise of Fishing with an Angle.* In this extraordinary tract, she reveals the arts of rod-building, line and hook-making, dressing flies and preparing baits. She tells us how, when and where to fish, warns us of the "twelve kinds of impediments which cause a man to catch no fish," and describes the eccentricities of individual species. She explains everything so accurately and so thoroughly that nary a woman in the past 500 years has bothered to rehash her basic advice, though countless men, of course, have made a career of it.

Following Dame Juliana's lead, female anglers have continued to gain ground on the good old boys for the past six centuries. Today, more women than ever are fishing. Judging from the number of women featured in the major flyfishing magazines, there must be a good dozen of us out there already. That is quite a comforting thought, for when I first started flyfishing, there were so very few women on the rivers, that I found the experience somewhat intimidating.

Within a matter of weeks, however, it became apparent that I was not only tolerated but actually welcome on the water. In those days I was 20 years old, tanned and thin, with straight blonde hair to my waist, and I suppose that accounts for some of the goodwill which was extended to me by the mostly male fishing community. In fact, I received numerous proposals of marriage during my first season after letting it slip that I could back up a pickup with a boat trailer attached. Now don't get me wrong here. You may have heard rumors about certain fishing femmes fatales whose antics on the river give new meaning to the expression "hooking fish." But that's not my style. I don't even wear lip gloss when I'm fishing. It's absolute hell on blood knots.

I have relatively few complaints about fishing with men. As a rule, I have found that men are extremely considerate to women anglers. They will freely dispense flies and information, and, until they realize you can actually fish, will cheerfully relinquish their favorite holes and allow you to cast from the front of the boat. Men are also extremely gracious and forgiving if you fish poorly. It's only when you fish well that they get truly upset.

A few years ago, I was invited to join two fellows who'd booked some time off to fish the Missouri. They were friends of a guide friend, and though we'd never met, I'd heard enough lies about the pair that I considered them ideal fishing companions. We introduced ourselves on the loading ramp at Craig, where the two gentlemen informed me they'd already run the shuttle, ordered the lunch and arranged to trade off rowing during the day. Nobody said anything about me rowing though the Missouri's a fairly easy river, but if they didn't trust me with the boat, I wasn't going to argue. I figured I could put up with a whole day's fishing if I had to. I started to climb into the back of the raft.

"Hold on there," said the fellow stringing up a Winston. "What do you think you're doing?"

"I'm getting into the raft."

"No, no," he said generously. "You take the seat up front."

They were nice guys, and I didn't mean to beat them up. It was one of those days when everything comes together, and I simply got a little carried away. I don't remember the particulars, but apparently I caught large numbers of fish. I recall making only one really bad cast, a 60-footer that was two feet this side of a voraciously feeding fish. Without thinking, for I never would have attempted such a thing consciously, I cocked my wrist, drew up the 60 feet of line, and, much to my surprise, set it down again in the feeding lane.

"Holy shit! I mean, Holy Dinah. Did you do that on purpose?" This from the guy rowing.

"No," said his buddy, reeling up to give me room to play the fish. "She just accidentally roll-cast 60 feet of line right onto the fish's head."

"That's right," I said, skating the fish across the

surface into the net. "I didn't mean to. I'm sorry." They exchanged a look of worried solidarity. I felt very much the outsider, an angling alien on some intergalactic fishing expedition, my identity just revealed.

As there were two of them and one of me, I decided to back off a little. When we pulled into shore, I remained in the boat while the earthlings fished the next hole on foot. Nobody twisted my arm to fish the hole, and I was quite content to sit in the raft, taking photographs of the two playing their fish and offering conciliatory congratulations. My companions were in considerably better spirits after taking a couple of fish each, nothing spectacular, mind you, but decent two- to three-pound fish. When they decided they could use a beer, I volunteered to deliver it. As I turned to open the cooler, a large golden back emerged from the weeds not 10 feet from the raft. A fish that big would have to be a carp, but I had heard that a carp could be taken on a dry and I thought it would be interesting to attempt.

I didn't bother to shake out any line. I simply detached the fly from the flykeeper, let it swing out over the water, and dapped it on the surface. A huge mouth seized the fly and kept on going. The three-pound tippet couldn't hold it. I didn't land the monster, but the gentlemen in the water got quite a good look as it streaked between them, spoiling their hole with a tailwalk.

"Big brown. Five, six pounds at least," was their judgment. "Made ours look puny."

"Holy Dinah," I said. "I thought it was a carp. My apologies."

To their credit, they didn't drown me on the spot. They were sportsmen, and at the takeout, they insisted that I accompany them again the following day. I protested vigorously, but they accepted none of my excuses, claiming they'd discussed it thoroughly and were in total agreement.

"On one condition," I said.

"What's that?"

"Tomorrow I sit in the back of the boat."

"The hell you will," I was informed. "You're sitting in the middle. Your turn to row. Be here at 7:30 sharp to run the shuttle, and while you're at it you can pick up the beer."

I don't usually fish that well, and I frequently fish quite poorly. Like many anglers, I am afflicted with a peculiar kind of fishing jitters that appears when the pressure's really on. Give me a howling wind or three current changes between me and fish, and I can nail the cast every time simply because the odds are against me and I don't put pressure on myself. But give me a reason to fish well — perfect conditions, an amazing hatch, huge fish everywhere, or prestigious company — and everything goes haywire.

The last time this happened, I was fishing the Snake River in Idaho. My host was the editor of a magazine I'd written a piece for, and needless to say, I fished like a dude. After missing my first dozen fish, I hooked my shirtless host between the shoulder blades, cast my reel into the water, and had to be rescued when I waded too deep. My first fish of the day was a whitefish, which my host seemed genuinely astonished to find existent in his river. My second was a cutthroat smolt which knocked itself senseless against the side of the boat.

My host was extremely gracious through all of this, tactfully switching the emphasis of the trip from fishing to nature. We lunched in a magical little side-channel where a spring creek comes into the Snake. In that place, the water is so clear and the vegetation above and below the water so luxuriant that you lose a sense of division between the two and feel that you are floating in a cool green sphere. The chill rising from the spring water helped to neutralize the effects of the 100-degree heat, and the afternoon went a little smoother. When we entered a canyon, my host began to scan the surrounding cliffs through his binoculars, promising me an unusual surprise. The surprise, which materialized after several hours of anticipation, turned out to be a pair of eagles. I didn't have the heart to tell him that in the coastal village where I live and teach, we go out at recess to shoo the damn eagles off our steps.

The next day I floated that section of the Snake again with a different party and brought several dozen fish to the boat, having abandoned the logic that fish living in fast water must be fast on the take in order to stay fed. However, my karma hadn't improved. The lodge shuttled our boat trailer to the wrong location, and it was a long walk out to the main road. None of this seemed to damage my standing with the editor, who continued to print my work, though he did shortly thereafter start an exclusive club for short, fat, bald fly fishers. I didn't take it personally.

Women often outfish men, and several interesting theories have been offered as to how such an outrageous thing could happen. "It takes skills, not bulging biceps, to land the lunkers," says *Bass'n Gal* founder Sugar Ferris, who believes that women may actually be better suited physically and emotionally than men to the sport of fishing. She points out that women have consistently scored higher than men on industrial tests for manual dexterity, eye-hand coordination and digital sensitivity, obviously important traits for angling. In addition, the qualities of persistence and patience help women to "fish slower, stay calmer, utilize rhythm, and be more methodical in their fishing patterns."

But Mother Nature did not forget the men when she handed out biological fishing advantages. I, for one, have always envied the ease with which male anglers are able to attend to bodily functions while fishing. The new neoprene chest waders equipped with fly fronts allow the male to capitalize fully on this natural advantage. Men should not despair when their female partners outfish them. A male angler with his wits about him can easily get two, three fish up on a woman while she is in the bush struggling with her waders.

A rather interesting theory for women's extraordinary success in salmon fishing is presented in *Salmon & Women: The Feminine Angle*, co-authored by Wilma Paterson and Peter Behan. As it turns out, the three most coveted British salmon records have been held by women since the 1920s: the biggest salmon on rod and line (Ms. Ballantine), the biggest salmon on a fly (Ms. Morrison), and the biggest spring salmon (Ms. Davey). Co-author Peter Behan, who has researched the non-feeding behavior of migrating salmon, suggests that either men emit some substance or chemical that repels fish and/or women emit a substance which attracts them.

Pheromone research is in its infancy. If the researchers do find a female attractant, no doubt we'll be gooping Madame X's with it and sprinkling it on cheese balls. In the meantime, if you're a male, I suggest that you book exclusively with female guides and wash your hands thoroughly before you go fishing. If you're fishing with me, kindly keep both hands in the boat, and the first guy who asks me to stroke his fly for luck will get a rod tip in the eye.

The whole issue of women outfishing men would not be problematical at all if men were not so competitive by nature. Men seem to have this thing with competition in general and with numbers in particular. As another female angler pointed out to me, the key categories seem to be first fish, biggest fish and most fish. I keep a journal of my trips, and I have noticed that when I fish alone, I will log "a couple" or "a lot" of fish, but when I fish with men, someone will have tallied up the exact number of fish and their weights or sizes, which I then record.

The first time I really clued into this numbers thing, I was fishing in the Yellowstone Park area. Technically,

I was on my honeymoon, having just married the guide who originally introduced me to flyfishing. A friend of ours had also come along. My husband and his buddy had been making an annual pilgrimage to the park for several years, and we saw no reason to exclude him from a major fishing trip just because we'd gotten married. Flyfishing has a way of transcending incidentals like marriages or even the dissolution of marriages. I am no longer wedded to the fishing guide, but we still fish together on occasion. If people are nosy enough to ask, we tell them that as part of the divorce settlement my ex was ordered to row me around on the river of my choice for two weeks every summer. I suppose that isn't very nice, but you'd be amazed how many people believe it.

We'd been hammering the Henry's Fork pretty hard for one or two fish a day, and the boys suggested taking a side trip over to the Yellowstone to lighten things up a little. At that time, you needed a fishing license to fish the park, but it didn't cost you any money. You simply informed the attendant when you entered the park that you intended to fish, and you were provided with a license. You also received a card on which you were supposed to record the number and species of all the fish you caught while in the park. We were given our licenses and surveys and were halfway to Buffalo Ford when our buddy suggested that I fill out the cards.

"Put everybody down for ... how about a dozen cutts and a couple of whitefish," were his instructions.

"Excuse me, but I think the idea is to fish first and fill out the cards later."

"Well, I guess that would be the normal way of doing it, but this is more of a challenge."

It was more of a challenge, and I suppose it was more fun, right up to the part where the boys were drinking celebratory beers in the car while I was still standing in the Yellowstone cursing the bats and the buffalo mites and praying to catch one more stinking whitefish.

Numbers aren't everything. A number may sound solid, but being a statistic, it's always open to interpretation. I wasn't exactly killing them last summer on the Green. I was fishing on foot one day near a takeout and had the misfortune to get in the way of an exceptionally loud angler congratulating himself on an 80-fish day. Perhaps I did experience an initial twinge of jealousy, but afterwards, when I'd had a chance to dwell, I mean think about it, I felt downright sorry for the poor fellow. I mean, the guy had floated seven miles of the Green River. At 7,000 fish per mile in Section A, he'd floated over approximately 49,000 fish. Allowing that a person can only fish one side of the boat at a time, he really only had an opportunity of catching half those fish, which is 24,500 of which he hooked 80, a percentage of .0032653 according to my calculator. Big deal. Of course, if I should ever have an 80-fish day, I suppose I could manage to tease a story out of it somehow.

It just could be that men and women fish from

different parts of their brains. I've just been reading *Dragons of Eden* by Carl Sagan, in which he makes the observation that sporting activities are governed mainly by the right brain. According to Carl, if you really want to throw off someone's tennis game, you get them involved in some kind of left-brain activity like describing to you exactly where they place their thumb on the racket. It seems to me that Carl may be on to something. I mean, plunk any of you pipe-and-tweed types into the middle of the river with huge fish rising all around, and what's the first thing you do? Calculate the speed of the water in cubic feet per second, record the water temperature, estimate the trout's window of vision and his sensitivity to the available light, calibrate your tippets down to four decimal places to eliminate micro-drag, and rattle off the Latin names of bugs. You can't get much more left-brain than that. Well, you dear fellows are free to do as you like, but from now on I'm going to fish from the right side — the female side — of my brain. The waters of life will swirl around me and images of primordial trout will fill my consciousness. Trout. Large. Fishing. Now.

Reading the Water

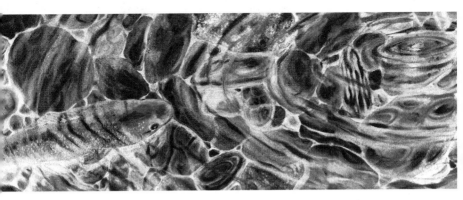

Part III

Riffles & Slicks

Yet the fish one remembers are not these noble creatures of orthodoxy and perfection but the unexpected fish, the almost impossible fish, that catch one with tackle and body off balance, and force improvisation and shocked, stumbling, cross-legged incompetence.

— Roderick Haig-Brown
"The Unexpected Fish"

Reading the Water

Why I Never Fish in British Columbia

MY BOYFRIEND AND I really got into it the other night. Fighting I mean.

"All you ever think about anymore is flyfishing!" he accused. "If you don't watch it, you're going to turn into one of those trout hoboes."

"Bums," I said. "Trout bums."

He just sighed and shook his head. John Silver's no trout bum. He owns a big hotel up here in northern British Columbia. The Last Resort rakes in a couple million dollars a year catering to rich loggers and commercial fishermen on government benefits. I figure that's not too shabby for a guy who doesn't know a roll cast from a double spey.

"It's a great mystery to me why you even bother to go fishing," he snapped. "You don't even keep the bloody fish!"

"I happen to be a strong advocate of catch-and-release fishing," I explained patiently, if quietly, this being a commercial fishing town.

The catch-and-release part is true. I was converted

to the practice by a flyfishing guide I caught and released several times one summer. Unlike fish, men do not always disappear obligingly when you let them go.

"And what have you got to show for all this catch-and-release fishing?" my boyfriend demanded.

"A clear conscience," I answered. "And photographs."

"Photographs?"

"Yes, I always take pictures of my trout before I put them back into the river."

You can see the trout are still alive in my pictures, because their little round eyes are looking down nostalgically at the water. Sometimes I question the morality of pulling the poor creatures around with hooks through their faces only to let them go afterwards. However, releasing a fish has obvious advantages over having to clean and cook one."

"At least you won't be going to Montana for the whole summer like you did last year," said Silver.

"I always go to Montana for the summer," I replied. "You know that."

"Montana? Across the border? Isn't that a bit risky?"

"Well, I suppose so. For one thing, they have sunshine down there, and you have to make sure you carry lots of number 39 sunscreen, especially on the water. Also, they can really ding you on the exchange nowadays with the Canadian dollar so low."

But that's not what he meant at all. He was talking about the violence, of course. You see, Canadians in an isolated coastal community like this get most of their information about the United States via satellite, beamed up from news stations in Detroit and Los Angeles. In their minds, the United States is just one big inner-city eight-lane freeway where people without proper medical benefits shoot each other quite regularly on a drive-by basis.

"Not to worry," I said. "I make a point of fishing under the overpasses where it's less crowded and out of the direct line of fire." No lie. Some of the best fishing (not catching) in the country is located under Interstate 15 on Poindexter Slough. *The Montana Angling Guide* has a nice picture of the very spot in their chapter on the Beaverhead. What they don't tell you is that those fish have been strategically placed as decoys to keep the dudes occupied while less gullible flyfishers catch all the more cooperative fish elsewhere.

I suppose there is some risk involved in climbing over those orange-painted fences they've got strung all over Montana, though in my case personal injury has been limited to punctured waders and insults to my femininity. Friends of mine have been shot at, or at least over, by rifle-toting ranchers, but that hasn't been a problem for me thus far. For one thing, I don't take up very much room, and I can disappear quite effectively behind a single clump of sage. For another, I'm a female, and most of my encounters with ranchers have ended in invitations to come on up to the house when I'm done fishing and have some lemonade because the wife will never believe an itty-bitty girl sneaked into the pasture just to fish unless she sees it for herself. One time I did get a real scare when a rancher actually stalked me for a good 15 minutes. Turned out he didn't mean to scare me so badly. He was just trying to get close enough to see if I really was a girl. Thanks a lot.

"Well, I just don't like the idea of a woman fishing alone, out there with all those men."

Personally, I've never considered that a liability, though I suppose all men are not as nice as the ones I've met. But perhaps there is some danger involved for any female fishing in a mostly male environment. Recently, a female friend of mine who had just taken up flyfishing was accosted by a flasher in a provincial park while practicing her casting. Afterwards, she joked that a more experienced caster might have taught the fellow a lesson he'd never forget; she also gave up fishing after the experience. I have too much money invested in flyfishing at this point to give it up, and I have never been hassled on the river. However, I do think it would be wise to take precautions in the future.

"Maybe you have a point there," I conceded. "Would you feel better if I embroidered 'Bobbitt' on the back of my fishing vest and carried a huge pair of nippers?"

"Well, I just don't see why you have to go all the way to Montana to go fishing. Why can't you just settle down in Prince Rupert and learn to fish like normal people?"

☞

We live in Prince Rupert, British Columbia, where

the mighty Skeena River empties into the Pacific Ocean. Like most residents of Prince Rupert, I am scared silly to drive along the Skeena let alone fish it. One wrong step on the Hawg Line hooked into a big chinook, and the Coast Guard would find me floating in international waters. Besides, the big salmon and steelhead patterns look like roadkills next to the size 16s I like to tie.

"Fish in Prince Rupert?" I asked. "You mean, fish for salmon and steelhead?"

"Why not? The Americans spend big bucks coming up here to fish."

"That's just it," I replied. "I only have light gear. It would cost a small fortune to outfit for salmon fishing. I could never afford it."

Silver just smiled and pulled out his checkbook. He signed his name to a blank check and handed it over.

"Tell you what," he said. "It'll be my treat. You try salmon fishing for two weeks, and if you don't like it, you can go to Montana with my blessing."

"Thanks," I said. "I'll give it some thought."

⌒

I headed over to the marine supply first thing in the morning.

"Excuse me," I said to the proprietor. "What can you show me in salmon fishing gear?"

"Why, you must be Mr. Silver's little friend," he said. "Silver said you'd be dropping by. I have instructions to give you everything you need and spare no expense. Now, what sort of boat did you have in mind?"

"Boat?" I asked.

"Well, you can hardly fish salmon without a boat now, can you?"

"I suppose not," I conceded, not wishing to appear argumentative. "What sort of boat would you recommend?"

"Well, I've got a little seiner that would be perfect for you. It's gonna cost a bit more than a gillnetter, but Silver said you'd probably think gillnetting was too hard on the fish."

"Right," I said. "I'd insist on taking the fish alive."

The proprietor nodded approvingly. "Fine. I can let you have the boat for around $400,000."

I started feeling seasick and took two Gravol. Maybe this wasn't such a good idea.

"Now," continued the proprietor, "How're you fixed for a crew?"

"Crew?" I asked.

"Well, sure. Silver tells me you're some kind of fishing hot shot. But you can't handle a boat like that all by yourself you know."

Crew, I thought. Highliners, deck hands, able-bodied seamen. I perked up. Maybe I'd get my sea legs after all.

"Top-notch crew. They'll work for a percentage or you can pay them up front; $100,000 ought to cover it."

"Well, okay," I said. Personally, I thought it was odd to have to pay people to fish with you, but maybe salmon fishing wasn't as friendly as trout fishing.

"Now what about a license?" I asked.

"As you know, a salmon license is pretty hard to come by these days. But seeing as you're a friend of Silver's, I think I could find you one for as little as $200,000."

I thought that seemed a bit steep for a license. No wonder my American fishing buddies were complaining about the new regulations.

"What does that come to all together?" I inquired nervously.

"With all the necessary equipment and provisions? I'd say three quarters of a million should do it."

I filled in the amount on Silver's blank check.

In less than a week, the crew and I were lounging around topside, carving scrimshaw and swigging rum. When Fisheries finally declared a 12-hour opening, we cruised out into the Pacific singing sea chanteys, set our nets, and pulled in a huge haul.

"Million dollar set!" hollered the mate.

"Really?" I said. "Maybe I'd better take some photographs."

The mate stood aside while I took pictures of the fish we'd caught with all those hundreds of fish eyes looking down at the waves to prove they were still alive. Then the hearty crew tossed all the fish back into the water and swabbed the decks.

Silver was waiting on the docks when the boat came in that night.

"So, what did you think of salmon fishing?" he

asked.

"To tell the truth, sweetheart," I said. "I thought it was a lot of money and bother just to go fishing. If it's all the same to you, I think I'll go to Montana after all."

"But darling," he protested, "I'll never make it through the summer without you."

"Cry me a river," I said. "A river I can flyfish."

Timing the Strike

BY THE TIME I TURNED 30, I'd realized two important things. One, I had to fish. Two, I had to work for a living. That's why I took a job at the Skeena Brewery in northern British Columbia. And that's how I came to attend this union meeting.

So far, so good. I've survived the reading of the minutes and two additions to the evening's agenda. I'm just beginning to wonder whether I remembered to apply the head cement to my last batch of steelhead flies when the committee chairman suddenly leans across the table and extends his hand. He doesn't look like a flyfisher. Dinger maybe. Definitely not a flyfisher.

"Mac McTavish," he announces. "I chair this union's bargaining committee. And you are?"

"Jessica Davidson. I'm new in the accounting department." McTavish makes the introductions all around. The other members seem to know each other.

"New blood, eh? What brings you up north?"

"Fish," I say. "Salmon and steelhead."

"Fish, eh? Don't fish myself. Get all the fish I need in the frozen food section." The others nod. "If you don't mind me asking, Ms. Davidson, what exactly is your interest in union politics?"

"I haven't the slightest interest in union politics," I confess. To tell the truth, the idea of attending a union meeting is about as appealing to me as hooking a whitefish in the eye. "According to my department head, I inherited a membership on this committee along with my new position. I'd describe myself as a moderate. I might be useful in balancing the radical element, though."

McTavish frowns. "Perhaps you'll change your mind after you've heard what our speakers have to say," he suggests. I promise to keep an open mind.

When the floor is turned over to the speakers, the meeting does take a more serious turn. Tempers emerge. I am hearing lots of language that would have come in handy when I lost my first steelhead of the season.

I really have no idea what they are going on about. I suppose I should be paying closer attention to the proceedings, but it's difficult to concentrate. After all, the peak of the steelhead run is just a week away. I glance surreptitiously at the cover of the fishing magazine in my lap.

There are photographs of steelhead, excellent photographs, in this magazine. There is an especially handsome fish on the cover. The picture captures the fish's size and a hint of its color and strength. But the photograph is nothing like the real thing, because hooking a steelhead is mainly a physical and not a visual experience.

Go down to the railroad tracks and wait for the next train. Cast to it and watch the line peel off your spool. That's what it's like to have a steelhead at the end of a fly rod.

You stand for hours, days, in the icy water waiting for the fish. First your fingers, then your legs, then your brain goes numb as you wait. You cast, you mend, you drift, you strip. You take three steps downstream and do it again. You do it a thousand times.

The first take sends a slow, solid pull up your arm that builds until it nearly wrenches the rod away. The pull draws you out of your numbed trance. The screeching sound you hear is the reel. You didn't recognize it, because the reel has never made quite that sound before. The fish leaps, silver and iridescent. The power you feel on the end of your line couldn't possibly be compacted into that sleek body. But it is.

You glance down. The line flying off the reel is a green blur, then a white blur. Fifty yards of backing are gone. Unthinking, you grab the line. It takes an instant for the pain to register, searing hot through your frozen fingers to the bone. You let it go. It goes. All of it. When you see the bare spool and the knot, you point the rod downstream. You brace yourself for the jolt. It is considerable, but nothing compared to the emotional impact of losing the fish. You are too stunned to be merely angry or disappointed.

You want it to happen again. The only problem now is time. It is November, and the snow has started to fall in the higher elevations. The steelhead season may last through December. Or it may end tonight. A blizzard followed by a rain could put the temperamental Copper out for the rest of the year.

☞

"Ms. Davidson! Davidson! You've got to make a decision!" McTavish glares and pounds on the table with his fist. "What's it going to be?" he demands.

"Huh?" I'm thinking of switching to the Green Butt Skunk, or maybe the Riffle Dancer.

"Which way do you vote? This committee is trying to decide whether to recommend a strike for the union. It stands at five in favor, five against."

I cast, I mend, I drift, I strip. I take three steps downstream and do it all again.

"We're waiting!" The others nod.

It is growing dark, and the snow is beginning to fall. Time is running out. There is a movement behind the fly, a miss, another slash. He takes it. I wait a heartbeat, watching him turn. My fist clenches tightly around the grip. Slowly I raise my arm.

"Strike!" I shout. "Strike now."

A Salmon Journal

September 15

Have decided to make Terrace the headquarters for this fishing expedition. Terrace, British Columbia, located on Highway 16, also called the Yellowhead. From Terrace, I can range along the Yellowhead west to Prince Rupert which the locals call "Rupert" and east to Prince George which the locals call "Prince."

September 16

Have been checking out the local shops and regulations.

According to all reports, there are plenty of fish in the Skeena drainage. The early summer fish, the sockeye, are called reds because they turn a deep red when they reach their redds or spawning grounds. In late summer, the pink salmon, which are gray-brown in color, begin to migrate up the Skeena. These fish are known locally as pinks, humpies, or just plain humps. The pinks are followed shortly by the coho, which are called silvers. Although these fish are silver when they begin their journey up the Skeena, like the reds, they turn red shortly after reaching the redds. There is a winter run of steelhead trout, which it turns out are not really trout at all, but salmon. When the weather turns warmer, the Chinook salmon, known as springs, kings, or tyee appear. These are accompanied by the chum salmon, which are called dogs. Semantic confusion aside, the angling sounds promising.

September 18

Spent the day checking out the Kitimat River. Lots of guys fishing from lawn chairs over there. Plant their rods in the gravel beside them and attach a little bell to the top to let them know when they've got a fish. Guess that's why they're called dingers, though I wouldn't say that too loudly around here. Pretty much elbow to elbow, so there was nowhere to run a fly line. Guys seem to have their own etiquette, though. Whenever somebody hooks a fish, the others reel up to give him room. Fellow hooked a fish this afternoon. The guy next to him had left his rod untended and gone back to the motor home to watch TV. They shouted for him to come, but he didn't. Another guy starts reeling up his line. Fellow comes flying out of his motor home, yelling about his rod. Grabs a gaff and sinks it in the other guy's arm. Mounties come next and take both of them away. Will keep looking for the ideal fishing situation.

September 20

Have discovered two excellent places to fish. There is the Lakelse, a river not to be confused with Lakelse, the lake. And there is the famous Zymoetz River, known locally as the Copper. Think I'll pass on the Copper, which is currently running high, cold, and muddy. Looks like tricky wading, the kind of river where they probably give you an organ donor card along with your Class I stamp.

Hiked along the Lakelse today, getting a feel for the river, chatting with the locals, and attempting to extract vital inside information. Have discovered a genuine character. Wears a bright orange survival suit under his hip waders, carries a two-handed spey rod, and sings to himself as he fishes. Just the type to know everything about a river. Sat on the bank today with his dog and watched him net four coho in a row.

So, how does a person catch one of those beautiful coho?

Ain't tough at all. Coho take a fly real good. Only problem is getting to them through all the bloody humpies.

September 25

Near as I can figure, humpies are the whitefish of salmon fishing. Incidentally, whitefish don't seem to be any more popular in Canada than they are in Montana.

The local limit here is 25 per day, and I've been asking why that's so high. Fellow I met on the river says that means you're supposed to catch 25 whitefish every day before you go home. Have been putting in some very long days.

Have never read about the humpies in the glossy magazines, but they're out there, zillions of them lying in the shallows, mottled gray and white, the males grotesquely humped. They are frayed and gelatinous. They look as if they would come apart in your hands if you picked them up. Supposed to be quite decent if you can catch them early enough out on the bars in the Skeena. But on the spawning beds, they are not a pretty sight.

Humpies are not especially spooky fish. Stepped on a humpy today when I wasn't paying close attention to my footing. The fish squirmed under my boot, and in my sudden panic, I took a dunking. Being the last week of September, the water was unpleasantly chilly. Have caught only three dead fish in my entire fishing career, all three in my first week of salmon fishing. All three were humpies, snagged off the bottom. Believe that is the real reason people fish with floating lines around here.

October 1

Have learned that coho show a slight preference for blue flies over orange flies. Have learned this by careful observation of other, more successful flyfishers. For myself, have discovered that coho snag readily on either blue or orange flies. Have begun fishing with lighter tippet, which enables me to break the fish off more quickly once I realize they are foul-hooked. Feel badly about leaving so many flies in the backs and tails of fish. My only consolation lies in the thought that these decorated fish may have some slight advantage in attracting a mate.

October 7

Have finally learned how to work my line, getting the proper drift and depth. The fish are starting to come up for my flies without snagging themselves. Got a good, honest take today. The coho jumped three, four times in its screeching run downstream. Bright fish, gleaming silver, 10 pounds. Learned that the light tippet I had switched to was not heavy enough to handle a fish like that.

October 14

Arrived at the logging bridge near the mouth of the Lakelse to find the area deserted.

Excellent. Last week the place was elbow to elbow. Now I've got it all to myself.

Rigged a rod and waded into the water. Two hours later, still hadn't seen a fish. Then it dawned on me — they've migrated.

Many back roads later, discovered the fish and the fishing community in the canyon section of the river. The fish had all turned red; there were precious few bright fish among them. The red fish were spawners, and I was reluctant to cast over them, even for trout. Coho season over for the year. Was gravely disappointed until I heard that a few early steelhead had been spotted downriver.

October 21

Decided to check out the steelhead reports on the river today. Ran into the character with the two-handed rod. Somehow, in among the spawning coho, he'd managed to find two bright steelhead.

So, how does a person catch one of those incredible steelhead?

Ain't tough at all. Steelhead take a fly real good. Only problem is getting to them through all the bloody coho.

The Adventures
of Brooke E. Trout

The Microscopic Optic

BROOKE E. TROUT IS RUNNING shuttle for John Boat, a friend of hers who guides out of West Yellowstone. John has the perfect physique for rowing boats, built long and solid from stem to stern with a wide flat bottom and arms as long as oars. John Boat eats like a Hebgen Lake Gulper and drinks like a fish. If he didn't row a boat all summer, he'd probably have a belly like a full-sinking line. But John Boat's a top-notch guide. And he's real popular with the clients because he packs lots of cold beer and carries a tape recording of the soundtrack from the movie "Jaws" which he plays whenever somebody hooks a big fish.

Brooke is on her way to meet John Boat right now, taking a shortcut down an old jeep trail that John told her about.

"Don't worry none about that little old jeep road,"

John said, sketching a rough map on the back of a bar coaster. "Road's good."

The old jeep road is like a bad video game. When Brooke isn't bouncing over corduroy, she's dodging windfalls. The woods are chock-full of thrill-seeking moose and grizzly bears. Every now and again, one of the critters runs across the road right in front of Brooke's vehicle. Brooke wisely brakes for the larger animals. But when little animals dart across the road, she pretends they're John Boat and speeds up, leaving a trail of carcasses behind her. Not one to waste an opportunity to stock up on fly tying materials, Brooke stops periodically to pick up a few prime roadkills. That slows her down some, and she is a little late meeting up with John Boat at the river.

"You're late, Brooke," John Boat drawls the words out, slow as a backwater slough. "Have some trouble on the road?"

"Nah. Piece of cake," says Brooke. "How was the river today?"

John Boat scowls like a bait fisherman fresh out of worms. "Terrible," he says. "Didn't see a fish all day. Real strange out there. Too quiet. Like the fish have been spooked right out of the river."

"That sounds bad," says Brooke. "Hop in. We'll discuss it over a beer."

"Afraid not," says John Boat. "Got to do some serious flytying tonight. See if I can solve this problem I'm having on the river. Got an important trip booked tomorrow, a real bigshot coming in to fish. The guy is heavily into that small-fly-big-fish stuff. You know, matching fish inches to fly sizes."

"Yeah, I've heard about those guys," says Brooke. "This year up in British Columbia someone claimed they caught a 28-inch steelhead on a size 28 fly."

"You believe it? What's the smallest fly you think a fish would eat?"

"Well, I don't know," says Brooke. "Some of the bugs that fish eat are pretty small, midges and such. I mean, even whales eat plankton, and most of that's invisible."

"I guess anything's possible."

"Guess so. I sure would like to see that guy fish, though. Any chance of me coming along?"

"I'd love to have you, Brooke," says John Boat. "Unfortunately this fella travels with a photographer and all his photo equipment. We'd be as crowded as the Big Hole during salmon fly season. Tell you what you could do, though. You could just happen to meet up with us on the river, and I could introduce you."

"Thanks, John. That'd be great," says Brooke. "Where do you pull out for lunch?"

"Valley of the Giants," says John. "See you tomorrow."

Brooke is waiting at the Valley of the Giants pullout at high noon when John's boat comes around the bend.

"There's a friend of mine," John tells the client. "Hey Brooke, any luck?"

"Not much," says Brooke.

"What kind of fly you using?" asks the client.

"Size 22 midge," says Brooke.

"Well that's your problem right there," says the client. "You're not gonna attract a decent fish on a roadkill like that. Got anything smaller?"

Brooke wades over to the men in the boat and opens her hand. "This is the smallest I got," she says.

"Where?" says the client. "I can't see anything."

"Course not," says Brooke. "It's microscopic. Minnow imitation with big eyes. I call it the Microscopic Optic."

"You're kidding me," says the client. "She's kidding me, right Boat?"

"No, she's not," says John Boat. "Brooke's one of the best tyers around. If she says she tied a microscopic fly, you best believe her."

"Well, it's a pretty amazing tie all right," says the client. "But will it catch fish?"

"Don't know," says Brooke. "I haven't tried it out yet."

"Well, what are you waiting for? Fire it on out there."

Brooke ties on the Microscopic Optic and casts her line upstream. A big fish hits it on the downstream swing, and Brooke's reel screams like a conservation society opposing the building of a new dam.

"Look, look!" yells the client, pointing at the smoking reel. "You're into the white!"

"I'm into the backing," says Brooke. "There's a hundred yards of dacron behind the fly line, you know.

Hasn't a fish ever taken you into the backing before?"

"Uh, sure. Lots of times."

About 50 yards into the backing, the fish surfaces, streaking across the water right toward John's boat with his mouth wide open. John's boat goes in the fish's mouth and out again through the gill so fast that John Boat forgets to open the cooler and turn on the "Jaws" music. The photographer, meanwhile, is pretty excited. He's got his tripod set up on the bank, taking pictures of the fish a frame at a time with the automatic advance on the camera clicking away, like you might photograph a moving train. He could have made a nice composite of the fish afterwards by sticking the frames together if he hadn't run out of film before the whole fish had passed him by.

"John Boat," says Brooke. "Suppose I was a client with a big fish on. What would you advise me to do?"

By this time, John Boat has recovered himself enough to crack a couple of beers and switch on the "Jaws" tape.

"Well," he says, "I reckon I'd ask you to make a decision about this fish right now. If you're gonna keep him for a trophy, don't take any chances. Play him as long as you want. But if you're gonna release him, you'd better bring him in pretty quick, before he gets too tired."

"What does a taxidermist charge these days?" asks Brooke.

" 'Bout 10 dollars an inch," says John Boat. "We're talking close to a million dollars for that fish."

"How about releasing him?" says Brooke. "You figure the four of us can hold him steady in the water long enough to revive him?"

"Maybe if we had us a couple of tug boats," says John. "Which we don't."

"I was afraid you were going to say that," says Brooke. "I guess I'll just have to break him off."

Brooke sighs, raises her rod, and jams the reel. The last they see of the fish, he's barreling upstream, throwing so much water up on the bank that the farmers don't have to irrigate for most of a week. Unfortunately, the client and his photographer get themselves tangled up in the trailing line as the fish roars by, and they disappear upstream with the fish.

"Well, ain't that just a cryin' shame," says John Boat, handing Brooke a beer. "That was one nice fish."

"Now, John," says Brooke. "You know it's not the fish we should be concerned about losing. It's the goddamn fly. I'm just not sure I can tie another one like it."

Night Fishing

" ... 498, 499, 500." BROOKE TOSSED the last fish into the back of the pickup and slammed the tailgate shut. Doc Spratley, the stream biologist, threw a tarp over the dead fish.

"Drought this year is really taking its toll," he sighed. "Appreciate your help with the cleanup, Brooke."

"No problem. Always ready to help out when a

river's in trouble."

"Speaking of trouble, I suppose you've heard that Dolly Varden's back in town. Word is your fishing buddy has fallen for her hook, line and twist-on."

"Dolly Varden?" scoffed Brooke. "What the dickens would Whitefish Bob see in her? She's so dumb she thinks the Henry's Fork is something to eat with."

"That's just it, Brooke," said Doc Spratley, "A man's got his fishing reputation to think of. Poor Bob never seems to catch anything but whitefish anymore, and you're out there hauling in trophy browns and rainbows one after another. Keep that up, you're gonna be fishing single in a double streambed."

"Fine with me," said Brooke. "Read my T-shirt: 'A woman without a man is like a fish without a bicycle.' I got better things to do than sit around painting my nail-knots waiting for some trout bum to phone."

"Just the same," said Doc Spratley, "if I were you I'd double-haul my ass down to Last Chance before that Dolly Varden character gets her hooks into Whitefish Bob. Hop in, I'll drive you."

It was nearly dark when Doc and Brooke pulled up behind Whitefish Bob's Airstream. Dolly's convertible, a pink metallic job with big tailfins was parked next to Whitefish Bob's jeep. Brooke crept out of the pickup and put her ear to the door of Whitefish Bob's trailer. It appeared that Whitefish Bob was trying to explain the dynamics of fly lines to Dolly.

"Weight forward ... fast-sinking ... sensitive response," Brooke heard him say.

"Oh Bob," giggled Dolly. "I just love it when you talk about flyfishing."

"Gag me with a trolling spoon," said Brooke. She pounded on the door, and Whitefish Bob opened it looking guilty as a poacher.

"Hi, Brooke. Something wrong?" he asked.

"Not at all," said Brooke, cool as a spring creek. "I just dropped by to see if you wanted to go fishing."

"In the dark?"

"Sure. Night fishing. You remember. Moonlight on the water ... browns as big as crocodiles."

At the mention of the big browns, Whitefish Bob's eyes lit up like flex-lites.

"That sounds great, Brooke! But what'll I do with Dolly here?"

"Any friend of yours is a friend of mine," said Brooke. "Bring her along. Meet you at the river in half an hour."

Brooke was waiting when Whitefish Bob and Dolly Varden came up the trail.

"I've already staked the place out," said Brooke. "There's a dozen browns lying tight to the bank up by the ranch buildings. Tricky wading, though. You go on ahead, Bob, and I'll take care of your little friend here."

"That's sporting of you, Brooke," said Whitefish Bob. "Sure you don't mind?"

"My pleasure," said Brooke. "Unless you want to stay here and let me go after the browns."

Whitefish Bob vanished like a spooled line.

"I don't know what you're up to," said Dolly, "but I ain't gonna give up Whitefish Bob without a fight."

"Whitefish Bob?" said Brooke. "What would I want with him? Half the time he's matching the aluminum hatch, and the rest of the time he can't catch anything but whitefish. He's all yours."

"You sure?" asked Dolly.

"I'm sure," said Brooke. "Hey, did you hear that?"

"Hear what?"

"Sounded like a bear. I'd better go investigate. I'll leave you the lantern so you won't be scared. Keep an eye on my purse will you?"

Brooke disappeared into the shadows. She wasn't gone a minute when Dolly heard something heavy coming through the bush.

"That you, Brooke?" Dolly asked timidly.

"No, ma'am. It's the Park Warden. I'd like to see your license, please."

"Well, I don't actually have a license," explained Dolly. "I'm not fishing. I just came down here with my friends."

"And who might your friends be?"

"Whitefish and Brooke Trout. I'm Dolly Varden."

"Right," said the Warden. "And I'm Moby Dick. I suppose you didn't know that it's illegal to angle for fish at night with a light. Hand over the lantern and the creel."

"Creel? This here is Brooke's straw purse. See for yourself. There's nothing in it but ..."

"Nightcrawlers. I suppose you didn't know that this is a restricted area. Flyfishing only. No live bait. And what do we have here? A gillnet and — there must be five hundred fish behind that rock!"

"I thought something smelled fishy around here."

"Sorry, lady, but I'll have to take you in."

"That's what you think," said Dolly, and she flipped herself into the river and disappeared in the whitewater under Osborne Bridge.

Doc Spratley took off his warden cap and scratched his head. "Sorry, Brooke," he called. "She was just too slippery for me."

Brooke stepped out of the shadows. "That's okay, Doc," she said. "We got rid of her, and that's the important thing. Thanks for helping out."

"No problem, Brooke. Catch you later."

"Nice fellow, that Doc Spratley," said Brooke as he disappeared into the bush. "I'll have to remember to send him a Christmas in July card."

The moon came up over the river, and the water glistened like the back of a golden trout. Brooke picked up her rod and headed up the trail in search of Whitefish Bob.

The Fence Pool Shark

BROOKE E. TROUT, FLYFISHING ENTHUSIAST, is having an excellent day on the river. Hooked 15 fish, landed 11. There is a good half hour of daylight left, and Brooke figures that's just enough time to head over to the Fence Pool to make it an even dozen. She wades downstream, fishing to an occasional riser, fishing a promising stretch of water, or just fishing the scenery. The big Montana sky, the osprey circling overhead and the clear spring creek are almost enough to make her forget about the hundred bucks she lost last night up at the lodge.

Brooke doesn't quite remember what happened. One minute she's winning drinks from some dude too drunk to hold a pool cue properly. Next thing you know, the dude is stone sober, and Brooke is woozily handing over crisp new pictures of presidents.

"Pool shark," Brooke says to herself. "I was hustled by a goddamn pool shark." Brooke rounds a bend in the river and stops dead in her Borgers. Speaking of the devil! If it isn't the hustler himself, standing in the Fence Pool and fishing to her fish! Brooke's blood boils like a scone in hot oil. A hundred bucks is just a hundred bucks, but a 20-inch rainbow is quite a different matter.

Brooke whips off her Western hat, and her waist-long blond hair tumbles down over her shoulders. The hustler nearly takes a header in the Henry's Fork.

"Hey, don't I know you from somewhere?" says the hustler, peering at Brooke with his beady, little split-shot eyes. "Weren't you over at the lodge last night?"

"Who, me?" says Brooke. "I just got here this morning. Drove all night. Couldn't wait to start fishing. This is my very first time. Fishing I mean, if you get my drift."

The hustler flashes Brooke a smile about as genuine as photo-dyed feathers. "So, how're you makin' out? Catch any?"

"Not a one. How 'bout you?"

"Eleven. I've been working to this fella for quite a while now. See him comin' up over there by the fence?"

"Sure do. Looks like a real geyser."

"Geyser? Oh, you mean riser. They're called risers when they come up to the surface real steady like that."

"Whatever," says Brooke. "I guess I'm just a little excited being so close to Yellowstone Park and all."

Brooke picks up the hustler's creel and pokes around in the grass hoping to scare up a rattler, but the little buggers never seem to be around when you need them.

"So where's all the fish you caught?"

"Oh, they're long gone. Usually I'm just catch-and-release."

"Just 'release' from what?" Brooke narrows her eyes suspiciously.

The hustler steals a quick look over his shoulder and gives a nervous laugh.

"It's just an expression, darlin'," he says. "It means you put the fish back into the water after you catch 'em."

"No kidding. I've seen dead fish floating in the water before, but I always figured that leeches got 'em, or pollution. I never figured fishermen were throwing 'em back."

"You got it all wrong, little lady. The fish are still alive when I put 'em back in the water."

"Even whitefish?"

"Even whitefish."

"Weird."

All the time he's talking, the hustler is making perfect casts over the trout. His fly lands six feet in front of the fish and drifts drag-free right over the fish's lie. As the big rainbow surfaces, Brooke can see the fly sliding up over the fish's head and down his back.

"Damn," says the hustler. "I've matched the hatch, and I've mismatched the hatch. I've made a hundred perfect drag-free casts right over that fish's head, and he just won't take. I give up."

"I bet I could catch him easy."

"Honey, if you can stick that fish, I'll give you 50 bucks."

"Deal," says Brooke, tying on a hopper. "Now, how do I work this thing?"

"Well fly casting's pretty tricky," says the hustler, climbing up the bank. "You gotta stop the rod coming forward and stop it again goin' back. That'll put some power in your cast."

Brooke steps into the water and shakes out her leader. Then she double hauls like crazy until all her fly line is out, and she's casting clear into her backing, about 80 feet with perfect loops.

"Like this?" she asks.

"That's the general idea," says the hustler sarcastically, "Except you're casting about 50 feet past the fish."

"Got to put it somewhere over the rainbow, eh?" says Brooke, retrieving her line. "How's this?" She measures a couple of false casts directly over the spot where the fish has been coming up just under the half-submerged fence. As she lets the fly drop, the hook point sticks solidly in the fence post that hangs out over the water.

"Uh-oh," says Brooke. "Looks like I'm snagged."

The hustler's lip curls back like a short shank hook.

"Serves you right. Don't suppose you'd care to up the ante?"

"Hundred bucks." Brooke counts back the seconds waiting for the fish to rise: five ... four ... three. Then she tugs lightly on the snagged hopper, which drops into the water just like a natural falling off the fence post. The fish turns and nails the hopper with a violent splash.

"Fish on," bubbles Brooke.

The hustler's eyes bulge like over-inflated float tubes. "One in a million," he says, shaking his head.

"Well, you know what they say. Even a blind hog finds an acorn now and again."

"You don't fish like no blind hog."

"I wasn't talking about me. I was talking about the fish," says Brooke. "That hog is totally blind in his left eye. You have to drop the fly on his right side just behind his good eye. Big splash usually gets his attention."

"Five hundred bucks says you can't break him off and hook him again," says the hustler, his voice slick as fly floatant.

"You're on," says Brooke.

Bait

WHEN IT COMES RIGHT DOWN TO IT, I suppose I'd have to admit that the main difference between fly-fishing and other types of fishing is the bait. I tie the odd fly, and secretly I'm proud of the flies that I make. I once showed one of my creations to a professional tier. "Humph," he said. "I guess it'll catch fish." Although my scruffy flies may not hold together as well as the professionally-tied flies, they do catch fish. I believe in scruffy flies. A friend and I once fished Slough Creek in August with a single hopper between us. By the end of the day, the fly had been reduced to a hook with a few wraps of string and one tattered turkey feather hanging from it, but it still caught fish. Later, the hook rusted, and the fly still worked. The rattier the better, as far as I'm concerned.

But up on the coast of northern British Columbia where I live, most people have never seen a dry fly, and they are usually impressed when I show them my fly boxes. I once showed my salmon flies to a friend of mine who fishes commercially. "Those are awfully pretty bugs," he said. "But I don't know why you go to all that trouble. Best way to catch a salmon is to soak a plug in bilge oil." Now, on the one hand, this makes some sense. Herring, which is used for bait, is a very oily fish, and lobster fishermen sometimes bait traps with nothing more than a greasy red cloth. On the other hand, Peter is the kind of guy who could cut off his head and keep a straight face just to get a rise out of you. I've never tested out his bilge-oil theory, but you're welcome to try. Bait is a very personal thing. It's your decision.

⌒ ⌒ ⌒

IT'S AUGUST, AND YOU'RE STANDING on the bank of the legendary Green River trying to decide where to begin. It's difficult to fish the Green. There are just too many distractions. As you hike along the river, you occasionally have to leap aside to make room for the mountain bikers who speed by, their legs flecked with green juice. They leave a carpet of plants, uprooted and shredded along the trail, mostly poison ivy and poison oak from the looks of it. They'll get theirs. And, from time to time, large parties of screaming yahoos on rented rafts drift by. On weekends, the locals say, you can park yourself next to one of the rapids in the upper river with a case of beer and witness spectacular wrecks all day long. The frog-men in diving suits, salvaging lost gear, are a much more interesting if incongruous sight. The float-tubers are clearly insane, and a few do perish each year. Then, there is the history of the place. Butch Cassidy's notorious Hole-in-the-Wall Gang once frequented the canyon. As you scan the cliffs for caves and other likely hideouts, you find yourself wondering if the outlaws fished. During the brief respites from other humans and their ghosts, you cannot help feeling overwhelmed if not assaulted by the beauty of the river. On the upper section, the red canyon walls rise straight up from Kool-Aid green water. The river is spring-creek clear, and phenomenal numbers of fish are visible to 20, 30 feet. Even in a wooden drift boat, you have the feeling that you're taking the glass-bottom tour. You could stand all day on the riverbank, staring into that aquarium, but you're here to fish.

You have heard that the Green River fish are tough customers. After all, they can probably see you at least as well as you can see them. They are shy and picky, and the selection of a fly is critical. It's been cooler than usual, and there are a few hoppers around, but they're still on the small side, and the guides say the fish aren't really on them yet. Still, you'd rather fish hoppers than just about anything. You capture a natural in the grass and pitch it out into the backwater, just to see.

Immediately, a nice brown comes up out of the current to take a look. He swims up on the right side of the hopper and bumps it with his snout. Twice. Then he circles the insect and tries to drown it from the left. The brown suddenly bolts for the safety of the current. Just when you think he's gone for good, he streaks back toward the hopper, grabs it, and disappears again.

You tie on a hopper pattern, cast it into the backwater, and give it a twitch. The brown swims over slowly, confidently, and takes the fly. And you thought those Green River fish were going to be tough.

☙ ☙ ☙

YOU'RE ALONE IN THE SHOP, and a guy comes in wearing a Western hat, very new blue jeans and polished cowboy boots. Town clothes. This is the genuine article, not a wannabe Eastern-type who doesn't understand that a real cowboy wouldn't be caught dead in faded denims off the spread. You recognize him. The fellow's a rancher who's rumored to have a few bucks and some very fine beaver ponds on his place. Matter of fact, some of the boys from the shop have been sneaking in there on a regular basis. According to all reports, the fish are big and difficult. It crosses your mind that maybe the rancher's got a complaint having to do with your buddies and orange-striped fence posts. But no, he's here to ask whether you tie custom flies.

Well, sure, what kind of flies does he have in mind? He leans across the counter and explains the problem, very quietly, though there's no one else in the shop. Seems he's got this pond on his place, and the kids have talked him into slipping a few trout into it. He was worried the fish wouldn't have enough to eat in there, so he got in the habit of throwing a couple scoops of dry dog food into the water whenever he fed the stock. Now there are quite a few trout in there, some big ones, too, but the kiddies can't catch them. The trout don't seem to be interested in eating anything but dog kibble, but when you throw that on the surface, they go completely nuts. It's pretty hard to get a hook through a piece of that dog food, and it doesn't last very long once it gets wet. The rancher doesn't come right out and say what he wants, but you get the picture.

You stay up all hours tying the flies, a variation on your standard cork beetle pattern, only square. Turns out, they work just fine, and the next time the rancher's in town, he makes a special trip out to the shop, buys a high-dollar fly rod, and invites you to fish at his place any time you like. In daylight. Your buddies are impressed as all get-out, wondering how you got on the good side of a guy like that. For the time being, you're keeping the details under your hat. The flies are kind of interesting, and you're toying with the idea of sending the prototype to one of the glossy magazines. With all the hatchery fish around, the Kibble King might be just the ticket.

⌒ ⌒ ⌒

You're ON SOME VERY CLASSY private ponds in Wyoming — underground springs, cress, persnickety trout — with a friend who is not exactly known for his subtlety or his reverence for fine water. In fact, he has the distinction of being the only fly fisherman you've ever known who can stomp audibly in waist-deep water. He has also exploded two perfectly good graphite rods that you know of by smacking them on the water after missing fish. On your last trip to the Henry's Fork, he hollered at you to get out of the water just as the Green Drakes started happening, just because the steaks he'd ordered in the restaurant across the way were done. And after lunch, you lost track of him on the river and caught him napping in the grass. You've never heard of anyone sleeping the Henry's Fork before.

Sometimes you wonder why you fish with a guy like that, but there are definite advantages. For one thing, he drives a souped-up Mustang convertible, late 60s vintage. While it's not much of an off-road vehicle, it does get you to the river fast. And he does get you on a lot of private water.

Today the fish are tough. It's hot and clear, and the water is barely moving. You're down to 7x, but your leader coils up on the surface, and even you can see how it casts a shadow on the sparkling gravel bottom of the pond.

Your friend is not fishing for the moment. He's sitting on the bank with a big fat grin on his face. He was fishing upstream a little earlier, doing very well by the sounds of it, and he's got this place figured out, he says. There's this one fly they can't resist, but he's going to let you try to work that out for yourself.

You're into the twilight zone of your midge box at the moment, down to the patterns you once bought in a specialty shop out of astonishment that anybody could or would attempt to tie anything that small. The fish wouldn't even look at the size 22 Royal Wulff fully-dressed, and you got a refusal on a little white, size 26 something or other. You're beginning to wonder if your friend's got a monopoly on that stomping trick, when he decides to take pity on you and disclose the secret weapon.

"I give up," you say. "Those fish have seen every fly there is."

"No, they haven't." He opens his hand, revealing the biggest, nastiest Electric Blue Leach you've seen in a long while, probably a size 2, but it looks a foot long after all those midges. "Go nuts," he says.

⌒　⌒　⌒

YOU'RE A UNITED STATES MARINE, assigned to the embassy in London, and a representative from the American Coarse Fishing Team comes by with a problem. They're scheduled to be in northern Ireland in a few hours representing the United States in the coarse fishing finals, and one of their team members has become ill unexpectedly. Is there anyone at the embassy who could fill in?

Your superior has heard through the grapevine that you're an avid fisherman, and he assigns you to the task. Your tastes actually run more toward trout than carp, but it's northern Ireland, and you've always wanted to see those chalkstreams, so off you go. It's only later that you get the real scoop on coarse fishing.

It seems this sport is done on stretches of water resembling canals or ditches more than streams. You fish with long poles and bait on hooks, but the really interesting part is the pre-baiting when the water is chummed with ground bait to create a feeding frenzy. Preparing the ground bait is an extremely important aspect of the sport, and the teams jealously guard their secret mixtures.

Although you have top clearance at the embassy,

you're not a regular team member, so you are not invited to be present when your team mixes their bait. From the chitchat around the place, however, you understand that one of the main ingredients is maggots. After the bait is mixed, it is locked in a special metal carrying case and placed in the van where you all will sleep on the competition site.

Carp you can tolerate. Maggots are a different story, especially maggots a foot away from your pillow. You're a Marine, but there are limits to the things you will do for your country. As soon as everyone else is asleep, you take the box outside and set it under the van.

Big Mistake. By morning, the box is missing. It's clear to your team that your bait has been stolen by a rival, who not only has the bait now, but the secret formula as well. You remind them that, as a Marine, you've been trained to kill with your bare hands, so they leave you alone for the time being. You volunteer to go check with the grounds supervisor just in case he happened to see anything suspicious during the night. You explain the problem to him, and he nods his head.

"So you're the gentleman who put the box under the van, eh?"

"Yes, sir. I am."

"That's not the kind of thing one does in northern Ireland."

Seems security got a little nervous when they spotted that metal box under the American van at 3 a.m. Security called the bomb squad, who very quietly jacked up the van, removed the box, and spent the next two hours carefully defusing the maggots.

⌒   ⌒   ⌒

THE THREE OF YOU ARE downright miserable. When you arrived in Craig, on the banks of the Missouri River shortly after sundown, there was a blizzard hatch of tricos in progress. The insects looked like snow in the headlights of your pick-up. They were drawn, as you were, to the neon lights in the window of Joe's Bar where, after a few, you saw something you'd never seen before or since: Spuds MacKenzie made entirely of tricos.

The guide friend who persuaded you to come on the trip promised excellent hopper fishing in August, but now that you have seen the tricos, you are prepared to allow for some flexibility in your plans. Perhaps you could fish tricos in the morning and leave the hoppers for later in the day. You could barely sleep in anticipation of the hour when those little black-and-white creatures would form into clouds, drift out over the water, and become trout food. By this time in your fishing career, you've gained enough experience to know that fishing success has less to do with skill than the trade magazines would have you believe. The most important thing is to be in the right place at the right time with the right bug, and then you get to see how stupid fish really are. But it's generally harder to do this than it sounds. The three of you figured that this was one of those rare occasions when you would hit it exactly right.

The next morning, you arrange to be in the right place, a backwater slough where the fallen spinners have collected along the foam line. Huge fish are slashing all around. The three of you are packing no less than a dozen trico patterns in sizes 18 to 22. You have heard that the Missouri is a bug factory, and now you believe it.

You have never seen so many tricos on the water. Their black and white bodies are pressed thickly together, creating a gray gruel of tricos half an inch thick. When your flies are cast, they land and sit on top of this soup. They don't even get wet.

You aren't even fishing anymore, just sitting on the bank and watching the huge fish cruising around with their mouths open. You imagine that this is the way baleen whales eat krill. Suddenly your guide friend is on his feet.

"It's August," he says, "and everyone knows that August is hopper month on the Missouri. I came to the Missouri to fish hoppers, and by gum, I'm going to fish hoppers."

He ties on a big one and slaps it down on the gray scum. The tricos part under the impact of the fly, revealing the first glimpse of real water that you have seen all morning. There is a river under there. And a fish, a fish coated with gray slime. A fish with a hopper poked through its upper lip. You are in the right place at the right time with the right bug.

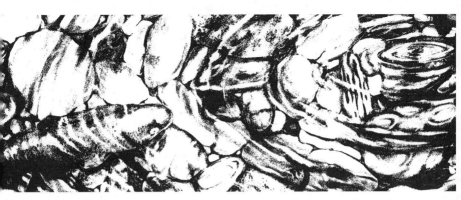

Part IV

Pocket Waters

The moving water of trout and salmon rivers, with all of the life found beneath their surfaces, touches me deeply. I am almost keenly aware of being where I want to be when I'm wading a river, fly rod in hand.

— Joan Wulff
"Where I Want to Be"

Reading the Water

Passion

FOR THE FIRST TIME in her 46 years, Helen Grady has time on her capable hands. She has used up the past two months of this time unpacking boxes, advising her lawyers and totaling her worth. Not her financial worth, which will be considerable once her husband's ranch had been appraised and apportioned, but her personal worth. Helen has concluded, and it is certainly the consensus within the community, that her husband Hank has committed a large blunder.

Helen believes (she knows!) that Angel will not be able to fill her shoes. She made a special trip downtown to have a look at this Angel in the boutique where the woman works. Angel is bony and overtly blonde with thin, pouffed hair and long red fingernails. Much perfume. Helen has difficulty picturing this vision rising at six in the morning to feed the hands, Helen's two grown sons among them, spreading manure in the garden, birthing the lambs. What can Hank be thinking?

It is not so much the other woman that bothers Helen, but rather, something that Hank has told the other woman about her. Helen has discovered one of Angel's love letters to Hank and read it.

Words cannot express how I feel. I thank you from the top, the middle, and the bottom of my heart. I thank you so much for the bracelet which I lost. It meant so much to me. Thank you for the knickknacks. Thank you for the artwork.

Artwork? It's not hard to see what Angel sees in Helen's husband. But what does Hank see in this person who is going to cost him a great deal of money and a solid 26-year marriage and who will prove rather useless to him in the kitchen, the garden and the barns?

We have been through so much together. How can you bear it, trapped in that lonely old house with your passionless wife?

This is the part of the letter that makes Helen angry, for she knows, as Hank knows, that she is not without passion. She is also fairly sure that Angel lacks the imagination to have thought this up entirely on her own; that Hank himself has described Helen to her in this way.

Helen's friend Roseanne thinks that Helen is being unrealistic about the whole affair, but Helen finds no consolation in the fact that other women tolerate this sort of behavior, and worse, in their marriages. Roseanne points out that Hank is basically a decent man, as men go. That, in the main, he has been a good husband to Helen and a good father to their boys, certainly a hard worker and a good provider. That eventually he will quit thinking with his male appendage and wise up about angel-face. That it's no picnic to be on your own at the age of 46. That Helen has more chance, at her age, of being struck by lightning, twice, or being killed by a terrorist than she does of remarrying. Helen wants to know whether she has a choice about this. She certainly does not intend to remarry, and she dislikes air travel. She does not tell Roseanne that she will take Hank back in an instant if only he will come to her and say, "Helen. You are a passionate woman. I lied to my girlfriend about you." She does not like the idea that she has become everything that Hank has asked her to become over the past 26 years, only to be pronounced "passionless."

Helen has been thinking a great deal about passion, and she concedes that there may be different kinds. She worries that Angel may be more passionate in bed. Helen has no way of knowing this, no way of knowing how sexually interesting she herself is, or Hank for that matter. Hank is the only man she has ever been with. Certainly, at the beginning, the two of them were passionate by any standard. Cody, their first, was born seven months after their marriage. They had been lovers right up to the end, and Hank's involvement with Angel had not seemed to diminish his interest in his wife.

If, by passion, Hank means dressing up on Friday nights, having a few too many and dancing the two-step in some smoke-blue bar, breaking up brawls in the parking lot afterwards and arguing over the keys before driving home, then perhaps she does lack passion. Angel may be more inclined to enjoy honky-tonks and to allow Hank to drive home drunk.

If what Hank means by passion is riding a horse until it's lathered, shaking, and bleeding from the nose, then, yes, she is quite and utterly passionless. Helen does ride — she can sit a cutting horse with the best of them — but never like that.

What Helen has in mind are quieter kinds of passion. Gripping the rails of the old brass bed upstairs and silently pushing their newborn sons from her body. Watching Hank sleep. Patching her great-grandmother's quilts, carried west by wagon. Cutting roses in the garden she has recently been asked to abandon. Watching the trout rising for insects in the evening in the river behind the barn.

It was curious, about those insects, Helen thinks. They seemed to come from nowhere. A fisherman had once explained it to her, a flyfisher he'd called himself. He had knocked on the door, asking permission to fish in their pasture, and she had granted his request. Hank normally ran the fishermen off, even the kids. As Helen understood it, there was some kind of dispute going on between the ranchers and the fishermen. But Hank was away buying stock, and Helen had seen no harm in it. She had watched the fisherman from the upstairs window. It had seemed so graceful, the way the line moved back and forth across the water, settled and floated, the way the fish bent his rod. She had put on a sweater and gone down to the river to watch him fish.

Thinking back, Helen recalls that these insects start out as worms — they have a special name which she forgets — on the rocks in the bottom of the river. The worms construct tubular houses made of tiny bits of wood and gravel. The fisherman told her of a river in Idaho where the worms pick up shiny bits of garnet to fashion their casings. Helen imagines a length of these abandoned casings, strung together, worn as a necklace. When the insects are ready to hatch, they drift up to the surface and shed their worm-bodies, emerging with wings.

The fisherman fished with a fly that looked like the insects that were hatching, cream-colored wings with a dark brown body. He had given her one of the flies. What had happened to it? Helen doesn't remember. She had put it somewhere out of sight, to keep Hank from seeing it. It will turn up eventually in the house, the house she doesn't live in any longer. The thought of Hank finding the fly amuses her. Will he know what it is? Will he think that she has taken up flyfishing without his knowing? Suppose she does take up flyfishing? There is no earthly reason why she should not, for Helen has time on her hands.

Helen likes the shop that she has chosen. She likes the name, *Frontier Anglers*, and she likes the way that the young man who waits on her assumes, at first, that she is one of these flyfishers. Her attention is drawn immediately to the bins of flies. She had no idea there would be so many, and she has located an assortment of flies similar to the one the fisherman gave her that night on the ranch. They are called caddis. She picks out a dozen, holding them in her palm until the young man brings her a plastic cup to put them in.

"You can't go wrong with those," he says, serious and enthusiastic at the same time. "These here are a bit bushy for my taste. I can trim them down for you if you like."

"That will be fine," she says. She waits, amused, as he snips a miniscule bit of hair from each fly. The trimmed flies don't look any different to her.

"Can we help you with anything else?" he asks.

"Everything," she says, and by the end of the following week, Helen Grady has been fully outfitted and graduated from flyfishing school. Hank will be surprised when next he visits his lawyers and discovers that Helen has requested fishing access to their ranch for herself and other novice flyfishers.

⌒

Helen understands that it is one thing to catch a fish with a guide standing over you and quite another to catch a fish on your own. She pulls on her waders and laces her boots. She fits the sections of her rod together and strings the line through the guides. She ties on a small cream-colored mayfly which she has learned is one of the appropriate flies to use midday on the Beaverhead. Though she has lived within 20 miles of this spot all her life, she has never before realized that Poindexter Slough is a part of the river which flows through her husband's ranch. She likes the idea that she may be standing in water which has flowed through their fields, though she has no idea whether the channels are connected in this way. She walks out onto the bridge adjacent to the parking lot and looks upstream and down. A fisherman joins her on the bridge.

"Fish here often?"

"No, this is my first time."

"You'll like it. Just spent the best part of an hour fishing around that first bend there. Ton of fish in there, but spooky. Too clear. They can see everything. I know better than to get suckered into fishing there, but I just can't seem to pass it up when they're rising."

"I didn't realize that the fish could be so difficult to catch in here."

"They are. Best bet is to get away from this section, off someplace where the fish don't see so many people. If you walk back on the track a bit, you can pick up a trail. Keep an eye on the weather. It's supposed to come down. Good luck to you now."

Helen likes the way that she is accepted so easily by the other anglers, the way they assume a connection with her just because of the rod she carries, the way they assist and guide her. She locates the trail without much difficulty. The narrow path leads away from the tracks through the high grass, not the kind of place you want to go if you aren't in the mood to see a snake. Hank would have had a fit. For all the times he'd set the boys on the backs of broncos and even bulls where they had no business being, he'd made sure they stayed out of the tall grass. Helen takes a deep breath.

The trail leads out to where Interstate 15 crosses the slough. Helen passes beneath the overpass and continues on, across a field until she comes to the river. It runs a little deeper here and faster, the water a sparkly blue rather than the flat, metal gray of the slower water. It occurs to Helen that she might have gotten past the slough and onto the Beaverhead proper.

She steps tentatively into the water and wades out carefully, as deep as she dares to go. The edges of the river are gravelly and solid, but in the weeds, closer to the middle, the bottom is softer, and she feels her way carefully. A pair of fish are rising on the opposite bank in the smoother water. She pulls out as much line as she can cast, but she can't reach the fish. Her casts fall three feet short of the trout, which continue to rise freely. She wades a few steps deeper on the spongy bottom, the long, trailing weeds catching on her boot laces, impeding her progress. Again, she begins to cast. Slow down, she reminds herself. Remember to wait on your backcast.

Her fourth or fifth cast reaches the fish. The fly rests briefly on the still water and, as the faster water in the middle of the river catches the line, it drags quickly over the surface. The fish go down, spooked by the dragging fly. Helen waits for them to begin rising again, but they are finished. She casts again, into the place where they had been rising, hoping to entice them to return. They don't. She decides to move on.

She turns back toward the bank and takes a step.

She cannot. Her right foot rises slightly in its position and will come no further. She probes the weeds with her rod, and they part, revealing her feet buried to the ankles, mired in the clay by the rocking motion of her casting. She transfers her weight to her left leg and, leaning away from the current, tugs with her right. She cannot move it.

Slow down, she says. Think. That would be the Jacobs' place, she realizes, using the interstate and the mountains to orient herself. If I stand here long enough, perhaps they will come into their fields, and I can attract their attention. She looks over their field, where the newly mown hay has recently been bundled and stacked. No, they are not likely to come today.

Her left foot is not as firmly stuck, and she finds that she can move this foot by working it back and forth in the ooze. Slowly, patiently she works the left foot until it comes free. She searches for a firmer footing and finds it on the gravel behind her. Again, she transfers her weight to the left leg and tugs. The boot comes free, and she topples ungracefully back into the river. She is in no danger. She regains her footing quickly and sloshes to the bank.

She has not dropped or damaged her rod. She tucks it beneath her arm and squeezes the water from her hair with her free hand, grinning. She has been baptized. She is mud to the knees, and spiky weeds trail from her boots. Helen likes the way she looks. The sun has disappeared behind a dark cloud, and for the first time, Helen notices the sky. Thunderheads. After the heat of the morning, it is likely to hail. She finds the trail and begins to walk across the field, briskly. By the time she reaches the overpass, the wind has come up, and a cool rain has begun to fall. A curtain of light flickers in the darkened sky on the ridge to the west, and she counts the seconds between the lightning and the thunder. One thousand one, one thousand two — not enough. She takes cover beneath the overpass, propping her rod against one of the concrete abutments. There is a flat plank spread across two rocks, the black remnants of a fire. She sits down on the board, her feet stretched in front of her. She can feel the water inside her waders, but it has warmed during her walk. She isn't really cold. The rain comes down in sheets on both sides of the overpass, less than a second now between the lightning and the thunder. The ground is dusty where she sits.

A small white fly appears on the surface of the slow-moving water. Suddenly there is a deep depression in the water around the fly, and it vanishes. This happens again. Helen leans forward to get a better look. A long, dark shape glides through the water in front of her. She has never seen a trout that large. There are several other trout in the water, slowly circling. She reaches for her rod, detaches the fly from the hook keeper and flips it onto the water. One of the cruising trout bumps her fly and leaves it on the surface. She casts it out again, sidearm, and, again, it is refused. There are more of the white flies on the surface now, many more, a flotilla of small white sailboats. She stands up, and the fish disappear. Spooky. Where have they gone?

The rain has tapered off somewhat. Helen looks upstream and between the drops, she can see the tiny white flies emerging from a spot where a willow leans out over the water. She sees a rise opposite the willow and then another. She steps into the water and wades to the edge of the overpass, peering out into the rain. She strips line from her reel and, keeping her rod low, casts straight upstream. She is unprepared for the take. At first she thinks she has lost the fish by striking too slowly, for it has come straight back at her, heading for the safety of the overpass. The large brown passes her going downstream, and she can see her fly lodged in the corner of the fish's mouth. She turns and connects with the fish at the end of his run. She plays the fish carefully, perhaps a bit too long, because she does not want to lose this first fish. When she has landed the trout, she measures him against her rod and releases him.

She is trembling as she takes up her casting position again. She casts upstream under the willow, but the fish have moved farther upstream. The rain is still coming down. What does it matter? She is wet already. She steps to the edge of the water, out into the open and begins to strip line. The air crackles with a force that lifts the hair on her neck; Helen feels her arm suddenly jerk and pitch her rod to the ground. She stumbles back against the concrete, crouching in the dust, her arms locked around her knees.

Helen thinks about her sons, hopes they have found shelter before the rain. She pictures Hank and Angel, sitting at her kitchen table, in that lonely old house a few miles away. Hank is sipping coffee and staring out at the rain. Angel has opened a bottle of red polish and begun to varnish her nails. Helen laughs softly to herself, without derision, a short and dismissive release. She leans out into the open and retrieves her rod. She stands and straightens. She wades into the middle of the slough and shakes her head, flinging the wet hair from her face. She raises her rod to the troubled sky and begins to strip line.

Dinner at Charley's

MONTANA WAS STRANGELY VERDANT that summer and unseasonably chill. The afternoon's torrents had ceased to descend upon the tiny borough of Craig, but the pools of standing liquid, an uncommon spectacle in that part of the arid West, were slow to relinquish their muddy tinge. Equally dampening to the spirits, my long-time fishing ally, Stephen G. Butt, registered Montana outfitter and proprietor of the Parrothead Fly Shop, was nowhere to be seen. A brilliantly plumaged if completely non-native specimen of Psittaciformes hovered above the white-washed door of his quaint shop. *Rio Sombra*, Stephen's handsome wooden dory, reclined peacefully in its trailer on the front lawn.

Well, he's not on the river, I surmised. I eased back into my vehicle of European design, ignited the engine, and proceeded a distance of some 10 yards. *Eureka!* I thought. *I've found it!*

Stephen's domestic vehicle was parked outside a local drinking establishment. There was little doubt that I would find my friend within, imbibing an aluminum container of ale.

Malerie! Stephen shouted, embracing me in a welcoming if somewhat ursine fashion. *Joe!* he cried, summoning the keeper of the roadhouse. *This gal's a lunatic about fishing. Last time we fished together, I had to forcibly remove her from the river. There was lightning like crazy, and neither she nor the trout had the sense to quit. Have a beer,* Stephen said to me. He was purchasing. *Unless you're in a hurry to get into your waders, of course. The caddis have been iffy, but they just might come off big time tonight.*

I'm not really prepared to fish this evening, I confessed, sitting down at the bar.

Relax! I'll open the shop and get you a license.

I have a license. I'm just not going to fish, that's all.

Stephen struggled with the idea that I was not eager to fish the evening Trichoptera. *I saw this coming,* he said finally. *It's Canada, isn't it?*

I won't deny it, I acquiesced. *Living in Canada has brought out the English in me, smoothed out the rough edges; I spell my first name with two l's now. I've discovered Roderick Haig-Brown and Ernest Schwiebert, and I've realized that there's more to this sport than fishing to the brink of exhaustion and gobbling microwave pizzas. I'm going to have a proper dinner tonight, even if I have to drive all the way to Helena to do it, and I'm not going to fish until tomorrow morning.*

All right, he agreed diplomatically. *I'm easy.* He was adjusting rather well to my new persona. *Dinner it is. So happens a buddy of mine has opened the Missouri*

River Lodge just this week. Charley Woods. Spent the past 27 years growing fine wines in the Napa Valley. He's got a Cabernet Sauvignon to die for, and he cooks a bit on the side for special guests. How does 8 o'clock sound?

Wonderful! I exclaimed. *Exactly what I had in mind.*

A caddis fly had found its way into the bar. It landed on top of my unsipped beer and folded its tent-like wings. Stephen rested his chin on his hands and stared wistfully at the insect. *What are friends for?* he shrugged.

⌒

The rustic lodge, situated at the spot where the Interstate 15 overpass crosses the old highway, looked out over the Missouri River. Charles had constructed it himself of native lodgepole pine.

Stephen was waiting beside his vehicle, and he had changed his shirt. *Nice outfit,* he commented as I approached his vehicle. It was a smashing outfit, a fitted cotton jacket in a pale blue and white stripe, a matching cocktail-length chambray skirt, and white shoes, elegant in a rustic kind of way, just like the lodge. I saw no point in telling Stephen that I could have had a new Winston for the price of that ensemble.

Shall we go up? I asked him.

We can't, he answered disappointedly. *Charley isn't here. He took two guys fishing today, and I guess they're still out. He wasn't really expecting us for dinner.* He leaned on the top of his vehicle, and suddenly his expression brightened. *Look!* he yelled. Caddis flies covered the top and sides of his vehicle.

Ordinarily, I would have been overjoyed to see the little beasts, but under the circumstances they signaled ill fortune. If Charles and his party had not reached the takeout before the Trichoptera started fluttering, they'd be into some rather decent fishing and might be reluctant to come off the water. *Hmm,* I mused, contemplating our options.

What would you like to do? questioned Stephen.

Why, we'll wait, of course, I instructed him. *We're flyfishers, quintessential patient types, are we not? And while we're waiting, we'll have a lovely chat. Tell me, old man, what have you been doing with yourself?*

Well, the Missouri's been tough this year because of the high water, he related. *Not much excitement fish-wise, but I did roll my car the first week I was here.*

Heavens! I exclaimed. *How did it happen?*

I was coming back late from Holter Lake, he began. *I'd been drinking coffee.*

And Grand Marnier and talking to that redhead behind the bar, I thought. *Were you injured?* I asked him.

No, but I did take a certain amount of grief from the locals until one of the other guides forgot to set the emergency brake on his Suburban and lost the whole rig off the boat ramp. They recovered the boat and trailer, but the truck's still out there somewhere, he reported.

You'd think they could locate a Suburban in the Missouri, I conjectured.

You'd think so, the Suburban being bright yellow and all, he confirmed.

A mini-pickup of foreign make pulled off the frontage road near where we stood, and two gentlemen got out. They wasted nary a second in rigging up their rods and setting white cowboy hats upon their heads.

Hot damn! exclaimed one of the chaps. *Ever see so many bugs?*

Let's get into our waders! shouted his companion.

No! yelled his friend. *The fish are in close! We'll cast from the rocks!*

They made their way quickly down to the river. While Stephen and I chatted, they fished hard, spending a significant portion of time extracting their backcasts from the thistles, tying on flies to replace the ones they damaged on the rocks, and regurgitating swallowed caddis flies. Never once did I hear the scream of a reel, though I heard several screams of protest pertaining to uncooperative fish. Above the commotion, Stephen and I could nevertheless hear the lovely little snapping sounds of trout mouths.

Stephen looked at his watch. An hour had gone by. *My guess is Charley's got himself mixed up in this hatch,* he hypothesized, brushing away the caddis flies which covered the front of his shirt. *Let's go somewhere else to eat.*

The hell, I said. *Do you think I came all the way to bloody Montana to feed my face? I'm going fishing.*

All right, said Steve. *I'm easy.*

I grabbed my rod from the car, clipped a pair of

nippers to my lapel, and slipped a flybox into the pocket of my designer jacket. I felt wonderfully light, and the flowing skirt was a welcome change from close-fitting neoprene. I scuffed the slippery soles of my new shoes in the gravel to roughen them up and crossed the road. The fish were tight to the bank, and there were plenty of them.

Evening, ma'am, said the dudes as we crossed behind them. *Evening, Butt.*

Watch your step on the rocks, ma'am, said Steve, *ignoring the look I gave him. If it turns out you like flyfishing, we'll get you some proper waders tomorrow morning. Now try a cast right over there. Just like I showed you.*

I held the rod high, sending the backcast straight up. The fly landed a foot ahead of the fish I had targeted, and he rose to it. I'd forgotten that the Missouri trout were sippers, and I snatched the fly away from him.

Good presentations ma'am, that's the key to successful angling, said Steve. *You set too quickly that time, but he'll come back. Try that again, same thing.*

I duplicated the cast and hooked the fish. The rainbow took line and would have taken more if I hadn't horsed him out of the feeding lane and into the backwater. I stood on the rocks, looking down at the trout below.

What are you going to do now? asked Steve.

What do you mean, what am I doing to do? You're the trusty guide. Get your butt down there, Butt, and release that fish so I can catch another one.

I did catch another one and several others after that. A number of cars screeched to a halt on the overpass above. I hope their pictures turned out. The dudes' luck never did improve.

What are you getting them on? they hollered.

Good presentations! I hollered back.

Are you trying to get me punched out? asked Steve.

I thought he might be feeling a little left out, so I handed him the rod and pointed to a large head well beyond my casting range. He took the rod and nailed a fish on a 70-foot cast.

Whitefish!

Well, think about it, Stevo. If you were a large rainbow and had a choice of being caught by a trout bum you saw every day on the river or a foreign blonde in a designer suit, which would you choose?

☞

Charley's party came off the water about the same time that we did. The veal piccata, with lemon, butter and capers was excellent. And though I blundered by requesting a light beer as a pre-dinner cocktail, I redeemed myself by ordering a 1985 Cabernet Sauvignon with dinner. During the meal, a single trico floated through the air and lit on the base of Steve's wine glass. He held it up to the light.

Look here, he said. *Good fishing tomorrow. I raised my glass to his. Just think of it,* he said, looking around the room. *Ernie fishes like this all the time.*"

Ernie who? I asked.

I got skunked the very next day. It rained all night, the water came up, and the wading was next to impossible for a lightweight like me. Though I was tempted to stay on at Charley's for the food and the company, I reluctantly made plans to move on. As I turned south onto I-15, I made plans to stop over in Helena for a little shopping. Something to fish the Ruby.

Definitely red. Strapless maybe, if the weather holds.

Note: With apologies to Ernest Schwiebert, of course.

The Emerger

SEVERAL YEARS AGO, AT THE BEGINNING of fishing season, I bought my 8-year-old son a light action spinning rod and reel. Anthony was already a veteran fisherman by this time, having netted sizable bass and northerns at his grandparents' place back East. My father ran a guiding service in northern Ontario, and anyone who ventured out in a boat with him was guaranteed to have a successful trip. Members of the immediate family were not only guaranteed but obligated to catch fish.

"Mum," said Anthony as we drove away from the tackle shop, "is this really my very own fishing rod?"

"Of course it's your rod," I said, a little irritated that he would ask. I was a confirmed flyfisher and hadn't touched a spinning rod since before he was born. I hoped, of course, that my son would eventually develop an interest in flyfishing, but I wasn't going to push him. Flyfishing isn't like that. Either it calls you or it doesn't.

We fished many of the lakes and rivers between Prince Rupert and Terrace that season, from tiny Lost Lake with its doubtful rowboats to the fast-flowing Copper River. Anthony fished with worms and briny-smelling gobs of salmon roe while I persisted in trying to raise trout to a floating fly.

Anthony enviously admired the stringers of cutthroat and Dolly Varden taken by the bait fishermen we encountered on rivers and lakeshores. He had almost given up trying to persuade me to keep the fish I caught, watching incredulously as I removed the barbless hooks and slipped the fish back into the water.

"But that's a keeper," he'd protest. "Why do you have to put him back?"

Because he took the fly so deliberately. Because he was a wild trout, not a hatchery fish. Because the exhausted fish came to my feet so quietly with none of the panicked, thrashing resistance that might have sparked some killing instinct in me. They were not the kinds of reasons that would have made sense to an 8 year-old.

Occasionally I took pictures of the fish I released, especially the dark-spotted cutts with the scarlet slash below the gill cover or the sleek bright steelhead trout. Anthony kept all of his regulation-size fish. We had an agreement that I would fish for picture fish while he fished for food fish.

Fortunately, the wild stocks were in no danger from my fish-killing son, who wasn't patient enough to be very deadly. His tolerance was limited to one netted fish, one lost lure, or one hopelessly-tangled line, whichever came first. After that, he was content to build luxurious toad habitats or holding ponds where he watched his captured sculpins swim until they found a hole between the rocks and darted away.

"They don't mind," he said of the imprisoned fish. "It's like a puzzle for them. It makes them smarter." At his age I'd constructed similar mazes, subjecting insects to treacherous obstacle courses and congratulating myself on their intelligent "escapes."

He shared my childhood enthusiasm for collecting caddis larvae or dragonfly nymphs, which he put into plastic bug boxes and scrutinized with a cracked magnifying glass. Occasionally he would extract a caddis worm from its cylinder and dissect the tube of gravel bits and bark, marveling at the strength of the silk that held the bits together.

Once he waded into the Lakelse River during a mayfly hatch to observe the worm-like nymphs floating up from the bottom of the river, emerging as winged adults on the surface. Together we watched the newly hatched adults drift across the surface to dry their wings for a few seconds before coming off the water. Later he sat beside me for hours as I tied nymph, emerger, and adult insect imitations on small hooks, advising me on their correct size and color for the waters we were fishing.

"I'd like to try that," he announced one evening. He was disappointed when I suggested he start with a much larger hook and an easier pattern.

Eventually Anthony fished with a fly I had tied. After the Kloiya River closed for the season, I lost interest in fishing, but Anthony was still keen on fishing the lakes. Near the end of August he decided to try his luck at a pair of tiny lakes outside Prince Rupert which were really better suited for picnicking than angling. There might have been some larger fish in their depths, but I secretly doubted that any really decent fish would live in lakes named Tweedledee and Tweedledum. Anthony fished while I picked berries nearby.

I could tell it was going to be a short expedition. Arriving on the marshy shore, Anthony promptly stepped into the bog, filling his gum boots with reeking slime. And he was rapidly using up his supply of worms, winging them right off the hook with vigorous casts or losing them to the minnows which boiled around his bobber like a school of miniature piranhas. He would have been prepared to call it a day when the worms ran out, except for several larger rings on the water's surface which suggested better fish.

I set down my berry pail and quickly knotted a trailing leader of six inches to a thumbnail spinner. I tied on a fly called a Muddler Minnow and handed it to him. He looked dubiously at the fly set-up but recognized it as a sculpin imitation and clipped it on the swivel in place of the bobber.

His ferocious cast plunked the spinner well on the other side of the rising fish. Reeling in rapidly, he tried to jerk the tackle clear of a clump of reeds as it came within four feet of the bank, but the spinner caught in the rushes. As Anthony tugged on the snagged spinner, the trailing fly flopped wildly on the surface. Suddenly a 14-inch trout sailed through the air, nailing the Muddler with an angry splash. The force of its impact freed the snagged spinner, and the fish was airborne a second time as Anthony horsed it out of the water onto the shore. The cutthroat was legal size and therefore a goner. I thought.

To my surprise Anthony picked up the fish, carefully removed the hook, and eased the trout gently back into the water. He watched it swim away and turned with an odd expression on his face.

"What an incredible fish! Did you see the way he hit that fly?" I nodded. "Do they always hit a floating fly like that?"

"They don't often sail through the air, but you usually see the take."

My son's hands trembled slightly as he picked up his rod and slowly reeled in the line. He took a deep breath and shook his head.

"Awesome," he said. I knew the feeling.

Reading the Water

Richard Said That

RICHARD AND I HAD FISHED together six times in six days. The first two days I'd floated him on the upper stretches of the Copper, because I thought that might be easier on him. But Richard didn't like being rowed around in a boat. I guess he wanted to stand on his own two feet in the river.

It was late October, approaching the peak spawning time for the steelhead that travel a hundred miles up the Skeena to their home rivers. The leaves had turned and fallen, forming a thick brown mat on the forest floor. The temperature most nights dipped below freezing, and the mornings were uncomfortably cool. Perhaps it was a better idea to be on our feet, walking and moving our blood around, than to be sitting, chilled, in a boat.

The Canyon Pool was ringed with anglers, as I knew it would be. Skirting the pool, my client and I walked downstream along the trail through the bracken fern and cedar. The muddy footprints on the trail ahead of us were frozen, and their edges crumbled under our felt soles. The trail led down to the water at a shallow place where it was easy to gain a footing in the river. We stepped in and waded another hundred yards downstream to a long gravel bar. In the spring, this bar would not have been visible, but this time of year its water-smoothed stones provided good access to the deeper runs.

The coho were mostly done, though a few still lay in the shallows. The gravel bar was heaped with the carcasses of dead fish, some decaying, others reduced to bleached bones. The stench of rotting fish was overpowering. I would smell it on my clothes and taste it in the back of my throat for days. There was one fresh carcass lying in the sand, still bloody with deep, wet tracks beside it.

"Grizzly," I said, crouching down to examine the tracks. "Look at the claws." The spiky imprints were a good two inches from the pad.

Richard looked at the half-eaten fish and shrugged. "Doesn't bother me," he said.

"A grizzly doesn't bother you? I thought you were here to minimize the stress in your life."

"I am," he said gruffly. "I'm flyfishing. Tweeds and pipes and nature. It got the doctor off my back. Don't you start." At first I thought he was kidding me, but then I looked up at him and saw that he was not. His dark eyes, already obscured by the swollen-looking pouches beneath them, had narrowed even further. The skin was stretched tight over his jaw. His free hand formed into a fist at his side.

☞

Richard had booked the trip from a hospital room.

He'd been in for tests. He'd complained of tightness in his chest, some trouble breathing. The doctors had discovered a problem with his heart and his blood, an excess of the hormone that caused the dark color above and below Richard's eyes. He'd insisted on the full explanation, and they'd explained the chemistry of it, the danger of cardiovascular exhaustion. It was the same chemical, they said, that played a role in the death of spawning salmon. Morbid as it seems, that's where Richard had gotten the idea of going fishing.

I'd had to juggle some trips to accommodate him, but Richard had made it worth my while, and he'd made it clear that my fee was a pittance. The man had done very well for himself down in Vancouver, well enough to buy himself a house in Point Grey, retire his folks on Saltspring Island, and send his kids back east to boarding school when he and his wife split up.

It was pretty hard not to be envious, about the money I mean. Out of nowhere the guy decides to take up flyfishing. Two days later, he's jetted into flyfishing mecca. In an hour he's on the river, his vest stuffed full of hand-machined boxes, waving around a split-cane rod and a limited edition reel. My life is fishing, and I'll never own an outfit like that.

Not that I'd want to be in the poor bugger's shoes right now. Richard and I are the same age, 38. I figure on running my camp for at least 20 more years. There's no way out of it, really. Not now. There might have been if I'd gone away to school instead of staying on to run my dad's fishing camp. I'd been offered a scholarship. I could have made it if I'd been willing to leave the river, if I'd been able to give this up. It seemed inconceivable at the time. Now I don't know. I've had some problems with my hands; the cold bothers me like it never did before.

Richard and I stood there on the gravel bar, and another angler came toward us, fishing through from upstream. I'd never seen him before.

"How's it going?" he asked.

"Haven't started. Any luck?"

"Got a nice hen up there on a dry. Made my trip." He grinned. "I'll go around. Leave you two this stretch. Nice rod," he said to Richard. He walked slowly down the bar.

There's a rapport among flyfishers, a settling into the feel of the river, a quiet respect for the fish and the sport. The first time I saw Richard with a flyrod in his hand, I realized he wasn't one of us. It had nothing to do with his being a beginner. He just wasn't easy. He seemed to lack a sense of his surroundings and his relationship to them. He had no restraint.

His cane rod was very soft and very slow. Richard strung the rod and began to cast. The line whipped back and forth and collapsed in piles around his feet.

"Ease up," I told him. He slowed down his casts, and sent his line in even, graceful loops.

An eagle flew overhead, low. Richard heard the rasp of its wings and turned to me with an uncertain look on his face. He opened his mouth to say something and closed it again. Richard didn't have any words for things like that. I don't mean he didn't talk. Richard was the biggest bullshitter ever. He had this way of just walking in and taking over. Back at the camp, he carried on long discussions with the other big-city clients, mostly doctors and lawyers, about investments and banking.

He'd talk fishing, too. In the short time he'd been fishing, he'd picked up an astounding amount of information. He knew his rod and line weights, his hook sizes and leader strengths, the record fish, anything with numbers I guess. But other things gave him trouble. He had no words for the iridescence of a sea-run fish, the foot-trailing flight of a heron, the cedar-stained flow of the river. Part of it was a lack of awareness, knowing what to look for and taking the time to see it.

I had begun to show him a few things, the way the fish lay on the deep side of a seam, the pattern of drift in a foam-filled backwater. He'd begun to wind down and notice the things around him. I had this crazy idea that I could save him, that flyfishing could change him.

⌒

The steelhead lay in deep water, farther out. We saw them, surfacing occasionally between the trunks of huge fallen trees on the opposite bank. There were still plenty of bright fish.

"Catch a steelhead," I said.

Richard waded closer to the fish and began to cast. The first day out he couldn't reach the fish with his limited casting range. Then he had trouble with the drift. He foul-hooked a few fish the fourth day, fishing deep. He lost his one fair-hooked fish trying to bring it in too soon. I'd brought along a spinning rod each day, as a backup, but Richard refused to look at it. I hoped he'd get a fish, because he was booked on the late flight to Vancouver. He'd already reminded me of it several times that day.

"What's on your plate when you get back?" I asked.

"Don't know. Go back to work I suppose. Don't really know anything else."

"Well, take some time to think about it."

"That's the funny thing," he said. "All my life there's never been enough time to get everything done. Now I've got nothing but time, and the thought of all those unbooked hours is almost more frightening than dying. What would you do?" he asked.

"If I were you?"

"No. What would you do if you had time? If I died tomorrow and left you a million dollars?" I glanced at him, to see if he was baiting me. Richard was concentrating on his line, and his face was serious.

"I wouldn't need a million. A hundred thousand maybe," I ventured. "I'd fix up the cabins and the boats. I'd replace the diesel generator and pay off the last of my bank loan." He nodded. "I'd spend more time fishing myself, maybe build some rods and tie a few flies. I'd take a trip in the middle of winter to someplace warm."

Richard looked at the split-cane rod in his hand.

That is the difference between us. He knows what he's worth. I know what I am.

⌒

The fish were tough. He had a couple of chases and refusals. At least he didn't put them down. They kept coming up, sailing out of the water like they had all the energy in the world. Richard was getting mad. He dropped his backcast on the gravel bar and broke the hook point.

"Better reel in," I said. "I think you nicked the hook."

"Shit," he said. He fumbled with the fly and had to retie the knot.

"Might as well check your leader."

"No time." He glanced back at the fish.

"They're not going anywhere. It only takes a few minutes. You're gonna be mighty disappointed if you hook a hawg and lose it to a wind knot."

"You do it," he growled, thrusting the rod at me." While I retied the leader, Richard paced up and down the gravel bar. I figured it wouldn't do him any harm to get out of the water for a while. It was cold, and he'd been standing up to his waist, not moving around much.

"How are your feet?" I asked.

"My feet? Think I'm some kind of candy ass just because I sit behind a desk all day?"

I shook my head. "Just checking. You're my client, remember? My responsibility. I'm supposed to watch out for you."

"I don't want your pity."

Where he got that, I don't know. I was only asking about his feet. When your extremities cool down, your heart has to work that much harder to get the blood around.

Richard fished for another hour. I was about to suggest we pack it in when he hooked a fish, a really good fish. It jumped three, four times and took him into the backing. He let it run, then brought it in, and let it run again. He handled it just right, finally beaching the fish on the gravel bar. Richard stood looking at the steelhead, a bright male. Fifteen pounds.

"Put it back." he said. He pulled his arms inside his sleeves and folded them across his chest. He lifted his shoulders to bury his neck deeper in the collar of his coat. Quickly, I revived the fish and released it.

"Let's go," he said. "I've had it."

We gathered up the rods and headed out. Richard wasn't very talkative. I understood. It was always disappointing to leave the river when you knew you weren't coming back for some time. Still, I figured he'd have been more hyped about landing that fish. I walked along in silence and didn't pay much attention when Richard lagged behind. Then he wasn't with me anymore, and I knew he was in trouble. I turned and saw him leaning against a boulder, breathing hard, his face the color of the stone. My shouts brought several anglers from the Canyon Pool.

⌒

They flew Richard to Vancouver the next morning. We kept in touch during his recovery. He was in remarkably good spirits for someone who'd just suffered a heart attack. He didn't blame me at all. He seemed almost relieved, as if he'd seen it coming all along and finally gotten it over with.

The last time we talked, Richard made me a business proposition. He'd done some research and determined that sport fishing was a growth industry. Salmon fisheries in other parts of the world, he said, were worth six to seven times the amount of the commercial fisheries. According to Richard, you couldn't argue with figures like that.

Maybe not. But an investment in a fishing camp bears close watching. I recommended a seasonal visit just to keep an eye on things, and Richard agreed.

He said he'd gone back to work part-time. Sitting at home was making him crazy. But he said he was trying to take it easy. When things got hectic, it helped to put his feet up, close his eyes, and imagine the tea-colored waters of the northern rivers. The tea-colored waters. Tea-colored. Richard said that.

Reading the Water

Fishing for Trout

I AM IN A NEW SHOP BUYING FLIES. The store that I usually visit is closed, which is disconcerting and a little puzzling. The shop's windows are lined with brown paper, and a sign says the business is changing hands. I didn't know the former owner well, but stopping at his shop had become one of my rituals. I'd pick up a box of donuts on my way over and sit, talking to the locals, over coffee. The shop had become a kind of gathering place for flyfishers and there was always someone interesting to meet. You'd hear who'd caught what and see a few flies tied.

I have just come off the river, a little disappointed because the pink fry hatch, which normally lures the cutthroat out of Lakelse mid-April, has not yet materialized. There is still a fair amount of snow around, and I narrowly avoided high-centering my vehicle on the drive out. The water is just 42 degrees. I learned this on the river from a fellow holding a thermometer underwater. I tend toward a more romantic assessment of angling problems and wouldn't carry a thermometer myself, though I don't mind having the information.

A bit of local lore suggests that when the alders green up, the alevins will wriggle out of the gravel, and the trout will migrate from the lake into the river. Most of these will be resident cutthroat, though there are rumors of sea-runs as well. Once or twice in a season you may catch a glimpse of an extraordinary rainbow, thick behind the gills and deep through the body, a husky fish so deeply striped with crimson that it looks hand-painted. There are steelhead, too, this time of year, long shadows that glide in and out of your field of vision, tense and sinister in comparison to the eager cutts. The steelhead add an element of anxiety, but they no longer figure in my fishing plans.

I learned to flyfish in the American West, and my tastes run to feather-weight rods and reels, miniature flies and cress-filled spring creeks. Men in this part of northern Canada laugh when I tell them I'd rather catch an 8-inch trout on a dry fly than a 10-pound salmon on a wet fly, but it's the truth. Still, when you live in northern British Columbia, it is difficult to ignore the salmon and steelhead if you want to be taken seriously as an angler. If you want to be one of the boys.

I am looking at the fry patterns and the Muddlers, and a young man has come over to help me. I ask him what he recommends for a fry imitation, and he shows me a silver-bodied minnow with a red throat and a length of mallard tied down on top and extending as a tail. It is a dozen-an-hour type fly, the kind of fly for which you automatically count out and barb a dozen size 10 hooks, snip a dozen tube bodies of exactly the same length, and strip the soft fibers from the shafts of your feathers in preparation. This type of tying no longer interests me, and I lay a half dozen of these minnows on my open palm.

The Muddlers are neither small enough nor sparse enough, so I will have to tie my own. I ask for a box of size 14 hooks and a patch of deer hair. That's kind of small to be tying Muddlers, but tying them small was one of the first pieces of advice I received about cutthroat fishing, and it has paid off over the years. The secret of tying Muddlers, fully-dressed, in a size 14 is to tie a dozen midges first, so the 14s will look large in comparison.

By the time the young man comes back, I have selected a very small Adams to use as a sort of pattern for the midges. "Oh no," says the fellow, "you don't want one of those. You were looking at the wet flies, and an Adams is a dry fly."

I consider telling him that I have been fishing for about 4 decades now, that I write regularly for several of the flyfishing magazines, that I guess I know the difference between a wet fly and a dry fly. Instead, I smile. I have brought this on myself, of course, by wearing a dress into a fishing shop. On the way back from the river I pulled onto a side road, changed into a pink silk blouse and denim skirt, combed my hair, and put on lipstick. I plan to have dinner at the Mexican restaurant I visit whenever I come to town. Joe Zak, a guy I often run into on the river, kids me every chance he gets about patronizing such a yuppie place.

According to him, a full meal deal at the DQ is a more appropriate dinner for a fisherman.

I pick out a few more of the small Adams, which are nicely tied. "You don't think a trout will rise to an Adams?" I ask.

The fellow opens a drawer of steelhead flies. "You know, there are steelhead in the Lakelse this time of year," he says optimistically.

"I don't bother the steelhead," I answer. "They have problems enough without people terrorizing them on their spawning grounds."

⌒

This is true, and quite a good rationale for laying off the steelhead at the top end of the Lakelse at least. But, in my case, it is a rationalization that comes after the fact. Up until last year, I did make a half-hearted attempt at steelheading. I invested in an 8-weight Winston and tied some very pretty flies. I hooked a few steelhead, but these were few and far between. What I remember most about steelheading is beating the water pretty hard for very few fish. I'd pick up the odd trout, of course, but even a decent trout was fairly boring on an 8-weight rod.

Each unsuccessful trip ended with a renewed dedication to make my annual pilgrimage south to blue-ribbon trout country. Celebrating 50-fish days in Montana bars with my American fishing buddies, I badmouthed the Canadian fish. On the basis of karma alone, I was hardly surprised that the steelhead would have nothing to do with me.

When I expressed my frustration to Rob Brown, a friend and fellow writer, he generously offered to float me down the Lakelse. I dropped my vehicle at Thunderbird, climbed into his truck, and, over the din of flying gravel and loud, complicated jazz, I picked his brain about steelhead all the way to the top of the river. The water was high, higher than I had ever seen it, higher than he had ever seen it. He broke a branch off a tree, pitched it into the water, and the river whisked it away.

If I were Webb or Whelpley, I'd have probably taken one look at the water and asked the guy if he was out of his bloody mind. I'd have chucked a couple stones in the water, cracked a beer, and stretched out in the sun. But I'm not one of the boys, so things were a little more complicated than that.

"Looks okay to me," I shrugged. There are no rocks to speak of in the Lakelse; a few sweepers, but Rob would know where they were. The raft got launched, and I figured I could walk out at Coldwater if I lost my nerve.

Things looked different once we were on the water, mainly because we were moving at the same speed as the water around us instead of standing still on the bank watching it roar past. I settled a bit. I understand about fishing from drift boats. It's what I've done every summer for the past two decades in Montana, Idaho and Utah. I stripped some line and mad a cast, tight to the bank, in a deep pocket behind a rock and ahead of a brush pile, the kind of cast you make on the Beaverhead all day long, a typical Beaverhead cast that would bring a huge trout streaking out for the fly. Rob frowned. "That was a dangerous cast," he said.

The only fish of the day was caught at lunch time. We were lounging on the grassy bank in the sun beside a feeder stream that reminded me of a spring creek. I was, in fact, describing the intricacies of spring-creek fishing when a large steelhead swam into the channel a few feet from where we sat as if to remind me of the trip's agenda. We watched it circle with the unhurried confidence of an unwatched fish, a rare glimpse of those things that happen on the river as a matter of course when we humans have gone home. The fish slipped into the deep pool in front of us. Rob handed me my rod and I hooked a feisty little rainbow that winged itself out of the water a half dozen times while I, distracted by its acrobatics, forgot to reel it in. It was a streamlined silvery slip of a thing, and Rob informed me that I had caught a steelhead smolt.

There were a few more mishaps. Rob took a dunking in a hole he had just warned me about. I wrapped a line around a snag in very fast water, and the line had to be cut to save the rod. The cheese buns got waterlogged. It was a wonderful day nevertheless. At the takeout, Rob shook his head in disbelief and expressed genuine amazement that the two of us had gotten skunked.

"I can't believe we couldn't find a decent fish," said Rob, who regularly logs more than a hundred steelhead a year.

"Speak for yourself," I said. "I caught a steelhead."

This season, I will not even make a pretense of fishing for steelhead. I have given away my Winston to someone who deserves it more than I do, retired it, in fact, for a sweet little 4-weight that I have always wanted to own. I am fishing for trout, and I do not feel the least bit apologetic.

The water has warmed up since last week. I have met up with Ed Chapplow on the river. I am fishing downstream of him, keeping well out of his hair, but close enough that we can keep tabs on each others' fish. Earlier today, on the lower Lakelse, Ed was fishing for steelhead, but now he is fishing for trout. I am nymphing just a rod's-length away, and he is fishing with no more than 30 feet of line out. Ed normally fishes the pants off me, and I am a little surprised that I am matching him fish for fish, though this is probably just because I am covering the newer water. We have each landed a dozen trout, and Ed is commenting that things are much slower than they were the previous evening. I look upstream to see whether he really means that a dozen fish is slow, but he is too far away to get a good look at his face.

I am fishing a drop-off. On my left, the water is shallow, no more than a foot deep, and on my right, there is a waist-deep hole. I am tossing the fly upstream and letting it drift over the ledge. I catch a glimpse of a steelhead in the deep water, and I get this quirky little feeling inside. I have seen a few today, but so far I have resisted the temptation to cut back to heavier line and attach a steelhead fly. I am fishing for trout. If the steelhead is agitated by my presence, he can go elsewhere.

The fish decides to make his move. He slips up over the ledge and into the shallow water directly in front of me, not 10 feet away. This is just where I have been drifting my fry imitation. I wait for the fish to move on. I glance downstream at Ed, who releases a cutthroat and immediately hooks another. I can't fish with the steelhead in my way, so I decide to run the leader over his head to spook him out of there. I flip the line upstream, and the fly drifts toward him. He opens his mouth, and automatically I set the hook. Amazing. Just like a trout. The fish does not react, and I doubt for a moment that I have hooked him. But when I raise the rod, very high, it bends quite sharply. Exactly six inches of fly line extends from my rod tip; the rest is leader. I bounce the rod a few times, but the fish does not react. I put my free hand on my hip and stand, glaring at the fish.

"What are you doing over there?" calls Ed.

"I hooked a steelhead," I say.

"Sure," he answers.

The fish hasn't moved, but it has begun lashing its tail a bit impatiently.

"I'm not kidding," I say. "I've got a 4-weight rod, 4-pound tippet, a size ten hook and a steelhead. I don't like the odds. Come over here with your net."

"Can't," he says, indicating his rod. He's into another cutt.

I wiggle my rod from side to side, and the steelhead finally feels the hook. He heads downstream, giving the reel a good workout just before the leader breaks. Chapplow looks up at the sound of the reel.

"I guess that really was a steelhead," he says.

With the steelhead out of my space, I am free to resume my fishing. For an instant, I consider clipping back my leader to a heavier strength, but there is virtually no chance that such a thing will happen again. I attach another fry imitation and settle down to the business of catching trout. We are up to three dozen apiece, and Chapplow is still complaining about how slow the fishing is.

The fly goes over the edge and swirls in the deep water. I catch a glimpse of color and set the hook. The fish responds with a tail-thunking splash which attracts Chapplow's attention. This time he reels up and sloshes toward me with his net. The fish obligingly heads in his direction, and I follow it upstream. We get a good look at the fish, enough to see that it is large but darkly-colored, very gooey. I point the rod straight at the fish and pull. Still, it was a steelhead.

"Are you living right or what?" Ed asks.

"No, I'm fishing right," I say. "I'm fishing for trout."

Chapplow decides that the fishing is definitely too slow. He'll take a break and come back in the evening when the fishing is a little better. I decide to keep fishing, and the fish deliver a very clear message. I get three more trout in all. The first is a large cutthroat.

Unlike the resident cutts, this one is large, silvery and fine-spotted. Maybe it is one of the fabled sea-runs. The second is a fat dolly, pink spots the size of dimes. The last fish, one of the hand-painted rainbows, comes straight up out of the water.

This calls for a celebration. On my way over to the Dairy Queen, I stop by the new fly shop. My waders have begun to leak, and the right leg of my jeans is soaking wet. My fishing cap has left a crease in my hair.

"I need some more of those trout flies," I say to the fellow behind the counter. "The wet kind."

He looks at me. "Chapplow was here a little while ago," he says, grinning. "And we have orders not to sell you anything."

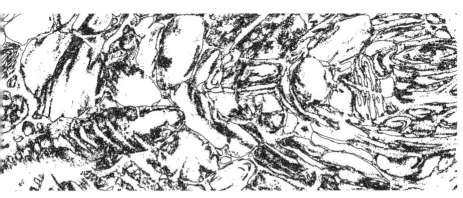

Part V

Tail Waters

The river was cut by the world's great flood and runs over rocks from the basement of time. On some of the rocks are timeless raindrops. Under the rocks are the words, and some of the words are theirs.

I am haunted by waters.

— Norman Maclean
A River Runs Through It

Reading the Water

Killing Fish

THIS IS THE STEEPEST PART OF THE TRAIL, a natural gully where a heavy spring runoff a few years back turned a traverse of short switchbacks into a scree slope, more or less. This is the part of the trail where Michael would slide a few steps ahead, establish his own footing, and extend a hand to help me down. Before I knew Michael, I never once hesitated at the top of this hill. The slope is exposed to the sun all day long, and I suppose I was normally cautious of snakes going down, mindful of where I placed my feet and my hands, but I had no fear of falling. Never mind. This is not about the steepness of any trail.

I am going fishing today, and Michael is not coming with me. His wife has asked him to make a choice, and he is going to stay with her because of the children. I agree it's the civilized thing to do.

Michael's children have been on my mind all morning. There is an older girl, 10 or so, slightly heavy and a bit of a tomboy with the loveliest auburn hair, her mother's hair no doubt. The younger girl started kindergarten this year, serious and quiet·like her father. You might think that I would feel some resentment towards the girls because they are Michael's children with another woman, but I don't. Whenever I see them I feel like touching them, just on the hand or on the cheek, places where they look like Michael. But, of course, they wouldn't understand this from a stranger, and I would never want to frighten them.

It is through Michael's children that we met. He had taken the girls fishing, and when their mutual patience had given out, they had wandered downstream and discovered this trail. At first I was annoyed to see them, hear them really, scrambling down the slope, shrieking each time they dislodged a clatter of pebbles, but their noisy descent was the worst of it. Once down, they sat quietly on the bank and watched me for a time, shushing each other and whacking their hands together in huge, silent claps whenever I hooked a fish. After a time I found that I actually enjoyed them being there, and when I decided to take a break, I sat down beside them on a boulder and offered to share my lunch. The older girl took a packet of chips and gave some to her sister.

"You fish real good," she said.

"I suppose I was showing off a bit," I said. "Thanks for being so quiet. You two like to fish?"

"We like it a little. Not as much as our dad. Our mother hates fishing. Major. She sits in the car and honks the horn about a million times when she wants to go. Mostly she makes us stay home with her. It's flyfishing, right?"

"Right." I thought about the mother, sitting in the car. Did she read, knit, what?

"My dad's got a flyfishing rod, but he can't make the line go out straight. He thinks we're bugging him, but we're not. He's just mad because he can't do it right. Maybe you could show him or something."

"You bring him down here, and I'll show him. He might not want to come, though," I said.

"He'll come," she said. "We'll bug him until he comes."

⌒

Michael must have been on his way already, looking for the girls, because the three of them appeared at the top of the hill in the time it took to repair my leader and change flies. At the top of the slope, Michael stopped and broke his rod down into two sections. Then he came down the slope very carefully, carrying the younger daughter in one arm, the rod in the other, and cautioning the older girl to stay behind him where he could break her fall if she started to slip. Michael was a little older than I'd pictured him, his vest and waders newer. At the bottom of the hill, he looked once up and once downstream to see for himself whether I really was fishing alone. He stepped closer to me then and shook my hand, taking it very gently as if to avoid bruising the skin.

"You must be the fishing girl," said Michael.

"And you must be the crabby father."

"They told you that?"

"No, that was just a guess. I used to fish with my father. When I was their age, I thought that trolling from boats had everything to do with the kind of trolls that live under bridges."

He laughed, too loudly, and both children turned to look at him and then at me.

"See?" said Michael's daughter. "You're getting happier already."

I kept waiting for the sound of a horn.

⌒

This is the place where Michael had his first lesson. It's the only decent pool on this creek, the only place where it opens up wide and flat enough to allow a backcast free of overhanging entanglements. Most people come here and cross immediately to fish to the opposite bank where there is some depth to the water, but I have discovered that the fish often lie in the shallows here, and if you make a careful approach, they can be teased to the surface with a waking fly.

This is not a very good place to fish, but it is an adequate place for a beginner to practice fishing, to learn something about the motion of the rod and the moods of the water in a fairly protected spot. I have only come here today because I lacked the energy to make the two-hour drive to the next good place to fish. No, I haven't come here hoping that Michael would join me. We don't fish here any longer. This creek is too close to town, and too many of the people we know hike and fish here. If Michael did come, it would mean that he no longer cares who might see us together.

But he will not come. Michael is devoted to his children, and for all I know he still cares for his wife. I don't like thinking about this, but I suppose it is best to face it. I am not a stupid girl, and I don't understand why I allowed such a complicated thing to happen. I suppose I didn't think it would end this way. I know that Michael was happy with me, but he was at a dangerous age, and perhaps I have been only a diversion.

In any case, it probably does not matter what I think, and in some ways, I am very much relieved. I am relieved because I no longer have the responsibility of worrying about Michael's children, and I am relieved because I won't have to kill any more fish.

You see, Michael and I used to take these weekend trips. We fished at a place a half-day's drive from here where the access to the river is owned by a rancher, and you pay to fish. There is a rod fee of $40 a day, a small price to pay to have a section of river to yourself. You leave your car at a designated spot, and the rancher moves it during the day so that by the time you have worked your way upstream five or six hours later, your car is waiting, and you don't have to backtrack.

Michael and I eventually became friendly with the rancher's wife, and one cool evening, when we had come off the river early, she invited us in for coffee. We sat on heavy mismatched oak chairs at a long, narrow harvest table in her kitchen, and she served us apple pie and coffee with cream from their dairy.

"Go ahead, now," she said. "Don't wait for me." She turned back to the counter as if to start another chore, and Michael got up, took her arm, pulled out a chair at the end of the table, and settled her in it.

"Sit," he said, his mouth close to her ear, his hands resting on her shoulders. Then he took her cup of coffee from the top of the stove and placed it in front of her. "When your husband gets home you can fuss over him. We'd rather just talk to you."

She sat there for a moment, smiling at him, more amused than pleased. "Where'd you find him?" she said to me.

"On a creek. I taught him how to fish."

"That's good, to have something you can do together," she said. "Harold's got his guns, and I don't care for that."

"The Ruby's one of the best trout streams in the country," said Michael. "You think you'd spend all your time fishing."

"Kids used to," she said. "Harold and I been busy making a living off this ranch the last 50 years. Now we're getting rich with folks coming from all over the country wanting to fish our pasture. You do that fishing with the things that look like little bugs?"

"Flyfishing. Yes, we do that. Wait a minute. I'll show you."

Michael went out to the car and brought in our fly boxes. He dumped them all out on the table, and we sorted them back into their compartments, naming the natural insects they imitated. We gave her a few to keep to show her husband. Her favorites were the tiny trichorithides.

"Yes," she said. "There's big clouds of these over the water most mornings."

As we were leaving, she put her hand on my arm. "Be happy, girl," she said.

That was the closest Michael and I ever came to doing anything together in public, and I liked visiting there with the rancher's wife, as a couple, though it was only pretending.

⌒

We had lovely days on that river, which oxbows through thickets of willows and stands of cottonwood over a bed of yellow gravel across the valley floor. The Ruby is a small river, never more than 20 feet across. It has all the features of a larger river collapsed into a smaller space, without those vast stretches of empty wading between the pockets of fishable water. The river is full of charming bends and fishy-looking pools created by the water-smoothed remnants of wooden fences and foot bridges, boulders and brush. It fishes best in gray weather, when the insects are hatching, and the fish do not cast shadows on the sandy bottom, and on those overcast days we would fish hard. But on the sunny days, when the browns were reluctant to show themselves, we would spend much of the day on a blanket in the shade of the cottonwoods, or we would sit beside the stream, sifting through the sand and fine gravel looking for the stones for which the river is falsely named. Actually, there were no rubies in the river at all. The settlers found some garnets and thought they were rubies. They made a mistake.

It was Michael who started killing fish. I had left him alone to fish one of our favorite spots, stepped out of the river and gone around him upstream to try the next hole. He was supposed to catch up later and leapfrog around me in the same fashion. Normally, he didn't like it when I was out of sight. He'd worry about me being off by myself and come looking for me after a short while, but that day he was slow in coming. I fished through the next hole with a dry, then fished it through again with a nymph, and still he hadn't come, so I went back to find him.

He was standing in more or less the same place I had left him. That's one thing I never managed to get across to Michael. Once you've fished through a hole and taken a fish or two, you've pretty well spoiled it, and it will be almost impossible to raise another fish without resting the pool for quite a long while. I stepped through the willows and there were the fish that Michael had killed, six of them, lying on the gravel. The largest was quite a decent-looking brown, a male about 17 inches. He had also kept a whitefish of some size. The others were browns, decreasing incrementally in size from about 14 inches down to six. I had not seen a dead fish in a very long time, and I had forgotten how different they look from live fish with their eyes centered, their colors off, and their bodies stiffened but not necessarily straight.

"My god, Michael," I said to him. "What is this

about?"

"I like to eat fish," he said.

"Six-inch fish?"

"That was the first one. I didn't know that I'd get another."

"And the whitefish?"

"The girls wanted me to bring something home for their turtles."

I felt something in common with Michael's wife just then because I suppose those were the kinds of ridiculous things he said to her when he came back from those weekends of ours.

"If it matters so much that she thinks you're fishing, why do you bother with me at all?" I asked him.

"It's not for her," he said quietly. "I'm protecting you. Someone phoned my wife and told her that I was not really going fishing." He pulled me toward him, and I turned my head away, but he turned my head back and kissed me quite seriously.

"I see," I said. And I did see, because I was the person who had telephoned his wife.

So we started killing fish, or, rather, Michael started killing his fish, and I allowed him to kill some of mine, at least the ones he saw me catch, because I was partly responsible. Calling Michael's wife was a childish thing to do, a desperate thing perhaps, but it was a necessary thing, and I did not feel sorry afterwards because it settled a few things for me.

And now it's settled completely, or it was, because Michael has suddenly appeared on the riverbank behind me. I don't know how long he has been standing there or how he came down the trail so quietly. He is clearly upset. Perhaps his wife has sent him away after all. That's what I might have done, asked him to make a choice just to see what he would choose and sent him packing anyway.

I stand my ground, waiting for him to come over, and then, seeing him walking towards me, I realize that I want to be with this man no matter what happens. He must see it too, because he is no longer afraid of what I will do. He puts his arms around me and touches his lips to my forehead. "I can't do it," he says. "I can't stand thinking of you out here all alone."

"What about your wife?"

He tips his head back and looks at the sky. "Don't ask me now. We'll work it out." Then he takes a sudden step backwards, and I can see that he intends to fish, so I get out of his way.

"I've just fished through here," I say. "Go on up ahead."

He shakes his head. "I'm fine. You go."

What I really want to do is stand there beside him, but I make my way upstream, far enough away to give him some room, but not so far that he is out of sight. We fish like that, the two of us, until the late afternoon sun goes off the water and the trout begin to rise in the shade of the willows. Almost immediately, I have a fish. I draw it up out of the weeds, a lovely creature, deep through the body with eggs, emerald-backed with a deep pink stripe and black, black spots. The colors are unusually vivid, spawning colors, and I think I must show this fish to Michael.

I walk towards him, skating the fish across the surface of the water at the end of my line. I know that I should not be doing this. One of two things will happen. Either I will lose the fish before I have a chance to revive it properly, or I will drown it by dragging it downstream. Either way, it is a dead fish.

Michael sees me coming and wades towards me. When he sees the fish at the end of my line, he smiles with one half of his face, and then he looks away. When he turns back, he says, "Thank you. I'll need some time."

You bastard. I reach down and twist the hook free. The fish struggles weakly to right itself, but cannot. The current takes it away, the last fish I will ever kill, but a fish I have killed for myself and not for Michael's wife. The trout floats away, an easy white target for a circling osprey which lifts it from the water less than 50 yards downstream.

I leave the pool and make my way up the trail. Behind me, Michael is still fishing, even though I have spoiled the pool by walking through it, and he does not have a prayer of raising a fish.

Reading the Water

The Firehole

Jonathan Miles Prescott III sat on the edge of his folding chair, waiting to feel something, anything that would bring closure to the six years he had devoted to the study of law. Pivoting in his chair, he scanned the audience where the members of his family were seated. As he suspected, the problem was not hereditary. His immediate family, at least, seemed capable of the feelings which eluded Jonathan.

His father was tickled pink under all that dignity, name-engraving proud of the son who would join the family law practice come September. His mother looked relieved, odd considering Jonathan could not recollect ever having given her a moment's grief; hadn't even scraped his knees until the age of 23, swerving on his bicycle to avoid colliding with a small child. On his final day of classes, Jonathan had been the last to leave the lecture hall. He had made his way across the varnished floor to the professor's podium and stood there looking up into the gallery of wooden seats and the leaded glass windows above, staring. Nostalgia, there it was on the face of his grandfather, who had also graduated from the stage where Jonathan sat.

"Turn. Around." The whispered directive came from Alison, on his left. Their surnames began with the same letter, and the two were frequently seated together at school events which required alphabetization. That is, in fact, how they had met. Jonathan faced forward and reached under his gown, producing a fountain pen and a sheet of yellow foolscap, folded in three. He wrote a message on the paper and passed it to Alison. *Last chance. Are you coming with me?* Alison flipped her head once to the left and once to the right. *Give me one good reason,* Jonathan wrote. Alison rolled her eyes, took the pen, and wrote in point form:

1. I hate fishing.

2. I hate rattlesnakes.

3. Wyoming is probably the Indian word for boring.

The fishing trip was Jonathan's graduation present. The expedition was his father's idea, the destination Jonathan's. The family had toured the Western parks, including Yellowstone, when Jonathan was eight years old.

"Off to fish the Firehole, are you?" asked his grandfather.

"I might. I hope to fish all the major rivers in the park, and the Firehole is certainly one of the more interesting ones."

"What a strange place that is, all boiling mud and geysers and that godawful smell. Signs every two feet warning people not to get off the walkways. As I recall, your grandmother had us all lined up on the bridge taking pictures. Couple of fishermen came up behind us and jumped right down off the boardwalk into the river."

"There's supposed to be a trail. I've been reading about it."

"Well maybe there is, but they didn't use it. When you saw them get into the water you wanted to go right in after them. Your father and I had a nice float trip planned for you the next day over on the Henry's Fork, and all you did was sulk the entire day and threaten to come back when you were all grown up and fish that stinking Firehole."

"I did?" The idea of having sulked and threatened as a child somehow appealed to Jonathan. He certainly had no recollection of anything except quiet compliance. A week later he was knee-deep in the Firehole.

⤳

Jonathan's preparations for fishing had not gone unnoticed in the parking area. He was photographed pulling on his waders against a backdrop of smoking fumeroles, having obligingly walked the hundred yards from his vehicle to the scenery. He had also attracted the lingering attention of a six-year-old whose arm was nearly extracted from its socket by his touristing mother who was apparently uninterested in the remarkable sight of Jonathan preparing to fish.

"Awesome," said the boy whose gaze remained fixed on Jonathan while his feet were hauled off in another direction.

Jonathan, succumbing to the effects of all this public attention, walked boldly out onto the bridge for a look at the river. One bank seemed completely normal. On the other, rivulets of steaming water oozed out of the earth and trickled down lichen-strained cracks over a crust of mineral deposits into the Firehole. A small crowd gathered on either end of the bridge, observing Jonathan. In the end, out of consideration for nervous mothers, Jonathan walked back through the parking area and headed for the river by way of the fisherman's trail.

The path appeared to be well-used. On the other hand, Jonathan reminded himself, vegetation in this climate did not exactly spring back after it was disturbed. Hundred-year-old ruts left behind by the wagon trains were still visible all over the West. A discarded gum wrapper restored Jonathan's faith in the footpath. Others had passed before him. Jonathan continued on his way, confident that the park service had deemed the trail safe even though a hundred yards away they had erected signs warning visitors not to step off the boardwalks.

To his satisfaction, Jonathan arrived at the river without plunging through the crust of the earth. He dipped the toe of his boot into the water with no ill effects. Then Jonathan lowered his entire left foot into the river. The neoprene above his boot registered no perceptible change in appearance or temperature, and Jonathan placed his right foot beside his left. He took a single small step and then a larger one. The river bottom beneath him felt solid. The hesitation between his steps gradually decreased until Jonathan found himself wading confidently in the Firehole River. He trailed his fingers in the water, finding it difficult to judge where the air ended and the liquid began. The water was bathtub-warm.

Straight ahead, in the middle of the river, Jonathan spotted a disturbance on the water. Moving closer, he observed a pod of small brown trout doing something on and above the surface. He hesitated to call it rising, because it was much more exuberant than that. The trout were erupting from the water vertically, exposing half to three quarters of their bodies before dropping back into the water. Jonathan had never seen trout behaving in this manner, and he immediately ascribed their behavior to the environment. At the same time, he realized that he had never actually expected to see any trout in the first place. Everyone knew that trout required extremely cool water in order to survive, and the Firehole was no spring creek. It seemed perfectly natural to him that trout living in the tepid chemical soup of the river would have to be damaged in some significant way, which accounted for their strange rise forms. Jonathan also reasoned that if normal trout were cautious, Firehole trout would be reckless. He moved closer.

The trout were on dragonflies, huge orange specimens with blue-black wings, the kind of dragonflies depicted in prehistoric scenes. These were Brautigan's trout, waiting for the dinosaurs to go away.

The dragonflies hovered above the water, just out of the trouts' range.

The largest fly in Jonathan's possession, an Orange Practitioner left over from a coho expedition, was half the size of the dragonflies. He tied it on and drifted it over the fish. They ignored it. No carrion eaters, the Firehole trout seemed to prefer live insects. Jonathan reeled in his line, waded close to the pod, and extended his rod. The Practitioner dangled over the water like a marionette without limbs. A half-dozen trout leaped simultaneously for the fly, as trout are apt to do in comic strips, and one managed to hook himself. Jonathan laughed out loud.

He inspected the trout carefully. It looked normal in all respects and darted quickly away when released. Jonathan sat down on the bank to celebrate his first fish of the trip with a cold beer. Normally, Jonathan would have looked around for a place to stash the remaining beer to keep it chilled until his return, later in the afternoon. But that hardly seemed sensible. Perhaps the drink of choice on the Firehole was a thermos of hot toddies. Perhaps the ideal time to fish the Firehole was the dead of winter.

Directly behind Jonathan, a jet of scalding water suddenly spurted from the earth. Jonathan hollered and bolted, abandoning his rod. Midstream he stopped and clutched his chest. The miniature geyser erupted for less than a minute, sending up a single hissing plume of water which collapsed back on itself, gradually diminishing in intensity until it resembled the flow of water in an ordinary drinking fountain. Jonathan waited another minute. Then he waded over to the bank and retrieved his rod. He peered into the smoking hole, now quiet, from which the jet had emerged. A puddle of water in a red-brown hollow was all that remained. Jonathan downed his beer, but drinking it felt less like a celebration and more like a reprieve.

Some distance later, the river divided, and Jonathan headed up the left channel. The farther he proceeded, the more ordinary the Firehole became. There were fewer signs of thermal activity, and the water temperature became cooler. The smell of sulfur was gradually replaced by the smell of sage and, eventually, of pine. The insects were smaller and less gaudy, the trout larger and more cautious. Jonathan took a pair of browns by floating a fly along the front edge of an undercut bank.

As the sun went off the land, Jonathan decided to explore just one more bend in the river before turning back. He fished that bend and two others before he found what he was looking for. The skeleton of an uprooted tree lay in the deepest curve of the bend, and a trout rose in the shelter of its partially-submerged branches. Jonathan stood quite still for a moment, planning his approach. It wasn't possible to float a fly through the tangle of sticks. Jonathan clipped off his fly, threaded on a single cylinder of lead, crimped it, and knotted on a tiny pheasant-tail. Stealthily, he moved into position against the opposite bank and slightly upstream of the fallen tree. As he raised his rod,

Jonathan glanced over his shoulder to check the path his backcast would travel.

A figure stood motionless on the bank behind him. It was a young woman, both hands pressed over her mouth as if to extinguish a cry. Jonathan took a step toward her, which caused her to shake her head vigorously from side to side. Briefly removing a hand, she pointed to the submerged tree and retreated out of range of his backcast.

The trout rose. Jonathan counted to three, measured the cast and delivered it. The nymph and lead hit the water well ahead of the branches and disappeared under the water. The line hesitated where the trout lay, and Jonathan set the hook, half-expecting the abrupt, dead-end tension of a snag. Instead, the line tightened with a kind of fluidity, and Jonathan connected with the fish at the other end. He steered it away from the deadfall and swiftly brought it into the shallows. The girl stepped into the water to look at the fish.

"Gorgeous," she said. "He's a hard case, that one."

Jonathan's hands trembled as he bent over to extract the hook. He was thankful for the growing darkness.

"Easy does it," he said. "There you go." He rubbed his hands together under the water and stood up, grinning.

The girl had taken her hands away. A dark stain extended over the girl's lip and across her cheek, blood. Near the side of the girl's mouth, the hackle and wing tips of a dry fly lay completely parallel to her skin. Jonathan stared.

"I'm afraid I've hooked myself," she said. She removed a pair of hemostats from a clip on her vest and handed them to Jonathan. "It's barbless," she said. "I tried to do it myself, but I couldn't get the right angle."

"God," said Jonathan. "You want a beer or something first?"

"Actually, I'd just as soon get it over with." She stepped nearer and closed her eyes. Jonathan pushed down on the eye of the hook and attempted to attach the hemos to the bend.

"I'm sorry," he said. "I'm shaking."

"It's not that big a deal. I'm not going to scream or anything."

"It's not you," he admitted. "I've been shaking ever since I hooked that fish."

The girl leaned over and laid her head on his chest. "It's the adrenaline," she said. "Your heart is pounding like anything."

They sat down together on the bank and shared Jonathan's remaining beer.

"You seemed to know that fish," he said.

"I've been fishing here all my life. I know almost all the fish," she said.

Jonathan felt that this was true. She would know them all, by habit, and by name, if such a thing were possible. For her, it would be possible. "I believe you," he said. He turned to look at her. It was too dark to see the color of her eyes, but he could see the white curve of her cheek; she was smiling. "How many times have you caught that fish?" he asked her.

"Many times," she said. "Hooked, but never landed. I can put a dry fly into that brush, but I can't get the fish out. I never tried a nymph. I'm quite impressed, actually, and a little annoyed that you caught my fish, if you want the truth."

Impressed, thought Jonathan. Why not? "I don't suppose that was fair," he said. "It wasn't really nymphing, I guess, with all that line out."

"I noticed," she said. "But you don't always have to go by the book. You're allowed to make things up as you go."

"Probably," said Jonathan.

"You don't sound convinced," she said. "I do what I like. Don't you?"

"I'm afraid I do what is expected," said Jonathan.

"Like what?" she asked.

"Like law. My grandfather was a lawyer, and so was my father. They're putting my name on the door as we speak."

"We could use some lawyers out here. Someone who cares about the rivers enough to take on the ranchers and the mining companies." She turned her face up at him, hopefully, he thought. He hated to disappoint her.

"I'm not that kind of lawyer," he said. "Anyway, it's settled. My office will be ready on Monday. In Boston."

"Where do you fish?" she asked.

"In Boston? I don't fish anywhere. I go on trips sometimes." He wondered what Alison would say about his trips.

"Why would you want to live where you can't fish?"

Jonathan sighed. "Let's get that hook out," he said.

"I'd forgotten about the hook," she said.

He attached the hemos and pulled straight back on the hook. It didn't come.

"You've got to really yank on it," she said.

"Oh god," said Jonathan.

He pulled on the hook once more, yanked, and it came free, still clipped to the hemos.

◠

They walked out together in the darkness. The parking area was deserted. They sat down on a picnic bench and took off their waders.

"I'd like to buy you dinner," Jonathan said.

"I don't think so," she said.

"You seeing someone?"

"No," she said. "I live here. You're one of the summer people, that's all. I meet a lot of people fishing, men mostly, and I've gotten older and wiser as they say. I know when someone's stuck."

"Stuck?" asked Jonathan.

"Sorry. Settled maybe. In their life, or someone else's life, just settled." She arranged her gear in the back of her truck. She climbed into the cab and rolled down the window. "Thank you anyway," she said.

"Last chance," said Jonathan. He had no idea how to stop her.

"Last Chance? Idaho? I wouldn't bother if I were you. The Henry's Fork isn't what it used to be."

"You're a scream," said Jonathan. His eyes were stinging and, for the second time, he was grateful for the darkness.

Jonathan sat on the picnic table long after the girl had driven away. He thought about the office he would occupy 20 floors above ground level in his father's building. He imagined cities with rivers flowing between the high rises, no trees for cover. He stood up and paced out the dimensions of his office on the bank of the Firehole. The desk would go here, the window facing the river. Equally impossible. Where was the nearest town large enough for a law office. Jackson Hole? West Yellowstone?

Why would you want to live where you can't fish?

Jonathan stopped pacing and loaded his gear into the car. He unlocked the driver's side and climbed in. He thought about Alison and her office in the adjacent building. His parents liked Alison. Alison did not like fishing. A familiar sense of detachment seeped into Jonathan's deliberations. A new moon rose over Firehole Basin, but Jonathan Miles Prescott III did not see it. He had fallen asleep in his rented car, contemplating his future.

Geoffrey's Wife

WE DROVE INTO CRAIG just as the sun was going down, which is quite late this time of year. I had wanted to stop earlier, around supper time, just outside Missoula. We have stopped there before, off the road in a small box canyon that is not a designated campsite. When we camp I like to have time to settle into the place, to get a sense of what it might be like to stop there for a much longer time. In Montana there are places that feel like they could be home, and that little box canyon is one of them.

My husband didn't want to stop. He was determined to press on, as he said. Geoffrey and I are retired now, and our time is our own. "Pressing on" could only mean something scheduled, and from what I could see of Craig, I'd guessed that we were going fishing.

There was not much to see: a general store, a bar, three tackle shops, a cluster of houses and the Missouri River a hundred steps away. This is Geoffrey's kind of town. It is not the kind of town in which he would actually choose to live, but the kind of wild Western town featured in the stories he will tell our friends, pipe lit, rye in hand, when we have gone back east for the winter.

I had never fished the Missouri before today, but Geoffrey probably has, and if he has, the trip will be recorded in one of the fishing journals that he has kept so meticulously for the last 50 years. His concentration isn't what it used to be, and for the past two years I have attempted to keep up the records of his trips. Geoffrey has worked out a formula over the years, and I follow his formula. The journal is just as he would have kept it except that it is in my handwriting.

I also do most of the driving now, and I am reasonably certain that I could maneuver our trailer into a parking site, but that is something Geoffrey still likes to do. Geoffrey backed the trailer into one of the serviced sites behind the general store and went to sort things out at the fly shop. The lights were on at the shop, but there didn't appear to be anyone inside. Geoffrey said the guides had probably just come off the river. They'd probably headed over to the bar for a cold drink and something to eat. Geoffrey had gone looking for the guides, and I went for a walk. I'd wanted to see a bit of the river.

In that section of the Missouri, several miles below the dam, the river runs clear and relatively slowly. A single-lane wooden bridge connects the town with the old highway which runs parallel to the river on the far side. The boat-launch sites are all accessible by this highway.

"No whitewater. Paved shuttles," Geoffrey had observed, pointing out the bridge and the highway. "This is a worn-out guide's dream." He'd said this unself-consciously.

I walked out onto that bridge, and illuminated in the headlights of an oncoming pick-up I saw what looked like snow. It wasn't snow of course but the evening hatch, dense clouds of mayflies and caddis. The insects were attracted to the white of my sweater and walking shorts, and within minutes my clothing was covered thickly with small fluttering bodies.

Up and down the river in the dark I heard fishermen calling to each other when they hooked or missed a fish. Occasionally a man would reveal his exact location by striking a match to light a pipe or switching on a penlight to tie on a fly. It was unavoidable that flies in that quantity would not be inhaled, and occasionally I heard fits of coughing accompanied by swearing and laughter down below.

I had never understood why large fish troubled themselves about tiny flies. At least it was clear to see why the Missouri fish would trouble themselves. It wasn't difficult to imagine the water below, its surface a thick soup of black and white spinners. The fish were working noisily, creating a boiling white rapid below the bridge where, in the morning, the water would flow smooth and slack.

"Geoffrey," I thought. "You have to see this."

But of course he would have seen it, here and on countless other rivers. He would have seen it years ago, long before I started fishing, when the hatches and the fishing were still unspoiled.

⌒

The guides had come off the river, and quite a number of them were in the bar as Geoffrey had predicted, downing a beer and having a late supper. Contrary to Geoffrey's theory the paved shuttles and lack of whitewater had not lured a bevy of worn-out guides to this place. With the possible exception of the weather-beaten ranchers in the corner, Geoffrey and I were the oldest people in the bar. None of the guides looked a day over 30, and most looked considerably younger.

I don't remember when the guides stopped looking like men to me and started looking like kids. Perhaps it was when they stopped wearing jeans with Western hats and leather boots and started dressing like the salt-water guides. These days they're wearing T-shirts and shorts, baseball caps and river sandals. There was something wilder, more appealing, about the Western clothes.

Geoffrey was sitting at the corner of the U-shaped bar, visiting with two young men from the shop he had booked with. They were both named Steve. One was a college student and the other, who had been fishing the evening hatch in his river shorts and sandals, was still shivering from the exposure. They were making a meal of a microwave pizza and describing to Geoffrey a successful party they had recently attended at which 11 of the 22 guests had thrown up. I wondered how they could talk like that and eat at the same time and how long they could keep rowing a boat eight hours a day on a diet of pizza and beer.

⁐

Steve met us at the launch site in the morning looking sober and well-fed. It was the college-Steve, not the hypothermic one. He was easily the youngest guide we'd ever fished with, and it felt strange putting ourselves in his hands, but he proved himself a capable boatman.

I have to say it was interesting to fish the Missouri. The trout traveled in schools called pods, and we drifted in the boat looking for these feeding pods. Usually we found only five or six fish feeding together, backs and tails circling like tiny sharks. But there were much larger pods as well, 50 fish on the surface feeding so voraciously they created a pocket of whitewater where there was none. If you spooked the pod it would disappear in a single sucking splash, the surface suddenly flat and calm. Flushing the toilet Steve called it, and I didn't care much for the expression.

I didn't fish at first. I sat in the back of the boat, the stern Geoffrey likes me to say, and I watched Geoffrey fish from the bow. Two people can fish from a drift boat, but I think it's easier for Geoffrey when he fishes by himself and he doesn't have to worry so much about hooking my line on his backcast or keeping his fly so far ahead of the boat. Normally he would have been standing, using the knee braces attached to the front deck, but he has been feeling a little unsteady on his feet. His balance is going now, and he has some numbness in his left leg.

Geoffrey was fishing with a fine old cane rod that caused the young guide's eyes to widen when he removed it from the case. Geoffrey's arms are still very strong, and he has always handled a rod well. Each cast was directed ahead of the boat, a reach cast followed by a quick mend. Geoffrey was so capable a caster, so obviously in control, that the guide did not at first perceive why he was missing the fish. The first time and the second I saw the guide lean forward expecting the strike, and when it didn't happen he sat back slowly and looked away to the other side of the boat. The third time he looked back at me, eyebrows raised, and I nodded my head pointing to my polarized glasses. The guide talked him through the fourth fish.

"Good shot. That'll get him. He's coming for it. There you go. Set." After that Geoffrey started hooking fish, and when he had caught half a dozen the guide turned to me and said, "He makes it look easy. Your turn, Mrs. Dalton."

"After lunch," I promised.

"C'mon," he said. "Your husband's getting the jump on you."

"My wife's not much for fishing from boats," Geoffrey said in my defense. "She can be persuaded to do a little wading from time to time if a guide knows a good spot."

Steve thought he knew such a spot.

"I'll never forget the first time she fished from a

boat," continued Geoffrey. "She was sitting in the stern, and she hooked a fish that went straight upstream. There she was, both hands straight overhead holding onto that rod, her feet in the air pointing straight out in front of her and her mouth wide open. And my buddy who's rowing looks at me and says, 'Do you know this woman?' And I say, 'Nope. Never saw her before in my life.'"

Steve looked back at me and shrugged, but it wasn't necessary. It never did bother me for Geoffrey to tell that story. I don't mind. Really I don't.

Geoffrey fished for another hour before the guide beached the boat on an island. After lunch, the guide suggested that we cross the island on foot and wade up the inside channel. Geoffrey said he would rest some, and after he was comfortably settled I went fishing with Steve.

He explained as we walked. "This is a different kind of fishing. The fish are lying on the gravel in fairly shallow water. The water is moving fast there, so when a fly comes over, the fish has got to make up his mind pretty quick if he wants it, and he usually moves fast enough to set himself. If you can manage a 30-foot cast, the water and the fish will take care of the rest."

Then he stopped and threw his arm across my path so abruptly that I ran into him. "Sorry," he whispered. "The big brown's in."

He took my arm and led me through the willows until we emerged at the tail of a backwater where the fish lay tight to the bank. A large boulder marked the head of the pool where the downstream current curled in to form the backwater. The fish lay behind the rock, taking advantage of its cover, the fast current on one side and the slow current on the other. We watched him take several flies on the surface, and then I reached to take Geoffrey's rod from the guide's hand. Steve shook his head.

"Not this one," he whispered. "It's just about impossible to get a drift over him. Your fish are just around the corner."

I held onto the rod, and he relinquished it. Geoffrey had been fishing with a hopper. I pulled a piece of tippet from a four-pound wheel and knotted it to the bend of the hook, adding a tiny pheasant tail to the opposite end. I stepped quietly into the water, silenced the drag, and pulled 30 feet of line from the spool. I made a long backhand cast into the fast water opposite the fish, throwing out plenty of slack. At first the line accumulated in a pile, and as the force of the current began to straighten the line out, the leader and the flies curled into the backwater. The trout took the nymph, turned down with it, and I set the hook. Steve was pleased when I landed the fish.

"Where did you learn that cast?" he asked.

"Watching Geoffrey I suppose, or maybe from a guide." When I first started fishing, Geoffrey would always take the guides aside and ask them to give me a few pointers and put me onto a couple of easy fish.

"I'm tempted to kill this fish just to see the look on his face."

"He'd think you caught it."

I released the brown, and we watched the fish take cover in the weeds.

"He doesn't know that you can fish like that?"

"Not really. I wanted to tell him a couple of times that I was finally getting the hang of it, but he seemed comfortable the way things were. And now I suppose it's better that he doesn't know."

The brown, fully recovered, turned into the fast water.

"Your husband was quite a sportsman, wasn't he? Just from looking at him, I'd guess he's the type that's fished from Iceland to Patagonia, probably been to Siberia hunting yaks or something."

"You wouldn't be far off either, except it was mountain sheep in Temlahan."

"And now?"

"His balance is going," I said, "and he has trouble with numbness in his legs. This may be our last season. I can't see Geoffrey allowing himself to be lifted into a boat. That will be the end of it."

"But not for you. You'll keep fishing."

And how was I supposed to manage that?

⁐

We told Geoffrey that I'd caught a fish. At the takeout he handed Steve a 50-dollar bill and shook his hand. Steve drove us back to Craig, and Geoffrey and I spent the early evening in the trailer. Geoffrey was very tired, and when he went to bed I went for one last walk.

From the bridge I could see the bar, its windows thick with mayflies. The bugs were attracted by the lights, and they clustered densely in the shapes of the neon signs behind the windows. There were so many flies and so many fish and out there in the Missouri was the big brown I'd released. I pictured him in the backwater hugging the undercut bank still too wary to feed. I thought about this being our last season. I thought about never catching a fish like that again, and I was just starting to drift off into some nonsense about the possibilities of going fishing on my own one day when the two Steves came out of the shop and headed across to the bar.

They are in there now with a pitcher of draft between them. When the hypothermic-Steve has stopped shivering he will tell the college-Steve about the dudes who visited the shop today and about the evening hatch, and the college-Steve will tell about the declining Siberian Yak hunter he guided today.

And perhaps, if the big brown has gained a reputation among the guides, he will also tell him about my fish. Then college-Steve will slap Geoffrey's 50-dollar bill on the bar and order a microwave pizza and another pitcher. God, I worry about those boys.

Bloodknots

I HAVE NEGLECTED TO TIE the wading boots properly, to pull the braided laces tight against the metal grommets, to fasten them securely with a double knot. This is partly due to a lack of effort and partly because the boots are much too big for me. They belong to my father. Belonged to my father. I suppose they are mine now. Neither my mother nor my sister fishes. I am the only one.

The boots are full of fine gravel which chafes between my thick, outer wading socks and the lightweight fabric of these summer waders. I should get out of the river to empty the boots, but it doesn't seem worth the effort of battling the current all the way back to the bank.

A mosquito buzzes close to my temple. I can hear its thin whine over the rushing of the stream, see the dark fluttering blur out of the corner of my eye. The insect lands and I feel its sting, such a tiny prick that I wonder why I have always made such a fuss about them, slapping at myself and smearing poisonous oil all over my face and limbs.

I slowly raise my hand to my temple and crush the mosquito. Not because I really want to, but because I feel I should. The same way that I felt I should wash my face and comb my hair and put on my clothes this morning, even though it seemed to make such little sense. It is unsettling, this doubting of routine, this absence of concern, this lack of energy. Perhaps I should not be here on the river at all.

⌒

"Go. Get out of the house for awhile," my mother insisted. She extended her arms and flicked her hands at me as though I were a bothersome child. "There's really nothing you can do until this afternoon."

My father died two days ago. The funeral is today at four. Mother is handling it pretty well. My sister is distraught, sedated. I am still waiting for my own emotion to surface in what I anticipate will be a sense of overwhelming loss. Every few hours, I test the depth of my grief, sounding its progress with tentative excursions into the past.

Earlier this morning, I sorted through my father's flyfishing gear. I have gear of my own, of course, but it isn't something you think of packing when your father has died suddenly and you are trying to catch a plane at an impossible hour. I sorted his flies and mended his leaders. I removed the spool from his old Hardy reel to change it over from a right-handed to a left-handed retrieve. I had to unwind all the line in order to rewind it onto the spool in the opposite direction.

The gear was spread out all over the kitchen floor.

A neighbor woman, who'd come by with a tray of baked goods for after the service, had to pick her way through the mess. Seeing the tangle of line on the floor, she offered to help. She held the line with a slight tension so that I could wind it more evenly onto the spool. She kept looking at the split-cane rod lying in sections near her feet. My father's name had been burned into the shaft in an old-fashioned, flowing script.

"This is beautiful old gear," she said. "Are you going fishing?"

"Yes."

"You're not," said my mother. She shut off the running water and turned, twisting her hands in her apron.

"You said get out of the house."

"I thought maybe a walk." She shrugged and left the room. I expected the neighbor woman to follow her. Instead, she motioned me to continue my winding.

"Do you think it's strange, going fishing? At a time like this, I mean?"

The woman hesitated. Then she leaned forward and said, very quietly, "Sometimes it takes a while to catch up with you. When Alex passed away, I didn't even cry. A couple of weeks later I was coming through the door with my arms full of groceries, and the wind caught the door, slammed it shut behind me. I put down the groceries, opened the door, and slammed it again. I must have slammed it 20 times."

I pictured the slight, gray-haired woman slamming the door, understanding her satisfaction with the final, solid sound of it.

The hatch is beginning. At first there is just a handful of bugs coming off the water, teasing a few eager fish into splashy rises. The nearest fisherman is a hundred yards upstream, stationed in one spot, not casting. Presumably he is waiting for the better fish to show themselves. He looks alert, expectant as the swarm of swallows gathering overhead.

I know this river. The hatch will gradually accelerate over the next hour or so, until the smooth surface of the water is frothed and silver with feeding fish. Until the air is both noisy with lunging rises and soft with clouds of pale-winged mayflies.

The upstream fisherman has his rod in the air now, stripping line with his left hand while the length of his backcast grows. I have picked out my fish as well, a trout that shows the curved half-circle of his back with each leisurely rise. The fish is directly across from me.

I drop a delicate Pale Morning a few feet upstream, floating it dead-drift over his lie. I am in the right place, with just enough slack in my line to ensure a drag-free float, but my timing is off. The bugs are hatching in greater numbers now, and it is difficult to focus on the rhythm of my trout with fish rising sporadically on every side.

One larger fish, in particular, is coming up just a rod-length away. His appearance is erratic, and his unexpected rises have twice startled me into lifting the tip of my rod, a reaction that makes the fly take a sudden skip over the water. Afraid that I will spook my fish, I decide to deliberately put down the erratic riser.

I face upstream, waiting for the fish to surface again, quickly stripping in my line until most of it lies in a tangle, bunched against my waist by the current. A cloud passes over the sun momentarily, and the water goes steel-gray. When the fish shows, I slap the line down hard on the water's surface just behind his head. The fish snaps up the natural that was his target, then lunges sideways, seizing my imitation and taking it down with him.

For a few seconds the leader disappears, its surface coils pulled straight down by the fish. Then, with a great sucking splash, the trout suddenly shoots through the air. He is coming fast, straight at me, eye level. His mouth is open, and I can see the fly lodged securely in his upper jaw. His gills are flared open. The fish is wide-eyed, and I wonder if he has seen me. He drops just short of hitting my chest, clumsily on his side, throwing water in my face.

The fish changes direction, runs upstream. The current does not appear to be much of a deterrent. The pile of line at my waist diminishes rapidly, and somehow I have the sense to let it go, to keep my hand off the reel. The last of the slack disappears, and the line slaps tight against the rod, sending out a shower of tiny droplets. For an instant I feel the weight of the fish connecting at the other end of the line in one strong pull, and then he is gone.

Damn. Damn, I want that fish. I lift the rod tip, aching for the fish to be there. I will play the fish carefully and bring him gently to net. I will hold him in the current, admire his colors until he is strong enough to swim away on his own. Instead, the line comes back easily through the water.

The fish will jump again, trying to shake the fly that is still hooked in his jaw. I will see the gleam of silver as his twisting body catches the sunlight. I stand looking upstream, but he does not show.

It is difficult to retrieve the line. My hands are shaking, and I feel weak, disoriented. The current tugs at my legs with a new intensity, as if the river has suddenly risen six inches. In turning, I lose my footing. My feet glide over the smooth stones and gravel bottom of the river, carried by the current. It occurs to me that if I fall, I will not have the strength to regain a footing. I concentrate on remaining upright, leaning into the current, angling slowly across the river toward shallower water and the protection of a small island. Slowly I make my way to the water's edge and sit down heavily on the bank, where I lie back in the rushes, my feet trailing in the water.

My father's death was sudden, unexpected. The secretary found him face down on his desk when she went in with the morning mail. It is difficult to believe. He was the sort of man you'd expect to perish on the side of a mountain heading for the continental divide. Or on the bank of an icy river during the winter steelhead run.

The sun is warm on my face. A mayfly, a survivor, crawls up on the underside of a reed and hangs upside down on its tip, swaying. There is a cold spot on my right instep where the gravel in my father's boot has finally punctured a small hole. It is just as well. If I get off the river now, I will just have time to drive back and change for the funeral.

I sit up and quickly untie the boots, keeping one eye on the river. I dump the gravel, rinse the boots, and retie the laces with a secure double knot. I repair the leader, adding lengths of fresh tippet with a series of secure blood knots. I carefully attach a new fly. The hatch could go on for hours. There are still plenty of fish rising. I wonder if my mother and sister will understand.

We thank the following for permission to use their words: Lyons & Buford for permission to quote from Roderick Haig-Brown's essay, "The Unexpected Fish," in *Fisherman's Spring*; Joan Wulff and Seal Press for lines from "Where I Want to Be," from *Uncommon Waters*; Simon & Schuster, Inc., for lines from John Gierach's *Sex, Death and Fly-fishing*; Scribner, an imprint of Simon & Schuster, Inc., for the quote from Ernest Hemingway's "Big Two-Hearted River, Part II," *In Our Time*; and the University of Chicago Press for a quote from Norman Maclean's *A River Runs Through It*.

To order more copies of

Reading the Water

Send $13.95 (U.S.A.) or $19.95 (Canadian), plus $3 for
shipping per order, to:

Keokee Co. Publishing, Inc.
P.O. Box 722
Sandpoint, Idaho 83864

Visa or Mastercard credit card orders by phone accepted
toll free at: 1-800-880-3573 from 8:30 a.m. to 5 p.m., Monday
through Fiday (Pacific time). For orders by phone, please
have at hand your credit card number and expiration date.